Viva Bloom's Notes

William Shakespeare's
Othello

Edited and with an Introduction by

Harold Bloom

Viva Books

New Delhi | Mumbai | Chennai | Kolkata | Bangalore | Hyderabad | Kochi | Guwahati

First Indian Edition 2010

VIVA BOOKS PRIVATE LIMITED

- 4737/23 Ansari Road, Daryaganj, New Delhi 110 002
  E-mail: vivadelhi@vivagroupindia.net, Tel. 42242200
- 76, Service Industries, Shirvane, Sector 1, Nerul, Navi Mumbai 400 706
  E-mail: vivamumbai@vivagroupindia.net, Tel. 27721273, 27721274
- Jamals Fazal Chambers, 26 Greams Road, Chennai 600 006
  E-mail: vivachennai@vivagroupindia.net, Tel. 28290304, 28294241
- B-103, Jindal Towers, 21/1A/3 Darga Road, Kolkata 700 017
  E-mail: vivakolkata@vivagroupindia.net, Tel. 22836381, 22816713
- 7, Sovereign Park Apartments, 56-58, K. R. Road, Basavanagudi, Bangalore 560 004
  E-mail: vivabangalore@vivagroupindia.net, Tel. 26607409, 26607410
- 101-102 Mughal Marc Apartments, 3-4-637 to 641, Narayanguda, Hyderabad 500 029
  E-mail: vivahyderabad@vivagroupindia.net, Tel. 27564481, 27564482
- First Floor, Beevi Towers, SRM Road, Kaloor, Kochi 682 018, Kerala
  E-mail: vivakochi@vivagroupindia.net, Tel: 0484-2403055, 2403056
- 232, GNB Road, Beside UCO Bank, Silpukhuri, Guwahati 781 003
  E-mail: vivaguwahati@vivagroupindia.net, Tel: 0361-2666386

www.vivagroupindia.com

Published by arrangement with

Facts on File, Inc.
132 West 31st Street
New York 10001
USA

ISBN 978-81-309-0471-9

All links and web addresses were checked and verified to be correct at the time of publications. Because of the dynamic nature of the web, some addresses and links may have changed since publication and may no longer be valid.

Every effort has been made to trace the owners of copyrighted materialand secure copyright permission. Articles appearing in this volume generally appear much as they did in their original publication with little to no editorial changes. Those interested in locating the original source will find bibliographic information on the first page of each article as well as in the bibliography and acknowledgments sections of this volume.

Published by Vinod Vasishtha for Viva Books Private Limited, 4737/23, Ansari Road, Daryaganj, New Delhi-110 002. Printed and bound by Anand Sons, Delhi - 110092.

Contents

Editor's Note

My Introduction is a tribute to Iago's diabolical genius as a dramatist who takes over Othello's other characters and stages his own play with them. Critical Views begin with the absurdities of the seventeenth century critic Thomas Rymer, who rejected all of the tragedy's characters as unpersuasive, a judgment shared by the Thomas Rymer of our century, T. S. Eliot. In contrast, the greatest of all literary critics ever, Dr. Samuel Johnson, justly praises the splendor of Othello's characters. Another great critic, William Hazlitt, beautifully describes the play's dramatic tensions, while S. T. Coleridge, despite his powers as a critic, errs in arguing that Othello was an Arab rather than a black.

A. C. Bradley, perhaps the last of the great Shakespearean critics, sees Iago's motivation as being a drive for power, after which Wyndham Lewis, as bad a critic as Thomas Rymer, outrageously reduces Othello to "the magnificent helplessness" of a bull confronting the matador, Iago.

The best of all American critics since Emerson, Kenneth Burke, writes brilliantly about the symbolism of Desdemona's handkerchief, while S. L. Bethell examines the matrix of diabolic images from which Iago emerges. For the poet W. H. Auden, Iago is a kind of experimental scientist, after which Stanley Edgar Hyman rather misleadingly sees Iago as essentially homosexual, and Leslie Fiedler regards Cassio as degenerating rapidly in the course of the drama.

Ruth Nevo imputes racial prejudice to Iago as one of his leading motives, while Susan Snyder subtly analyzes Desdemona's love for Othello, and John Bayley examines the sexual uneasiness of all the males in the play. In an accurate feminist critique, Carol Thomas Neely shows the moral superiority of the women over the men in Othello, after which the superb poet Anthony Hecht reflects brilliantly upon Othello's Christianity, and Edward Berry treats the effect upon Othello of racial prejudice.

Julia Genster shrewdly analyzes the affinities between military rank and sexual power in the play, while Derek Cohen illuminates the vexed question of Othello's suicide. In a final extract, James R. Aubrey explores the social background of the racial attitudes of Venice in the play, by relating those attitudes to the Renaissance popular imagination in regard to blacks.

Introduction

HAROLD BLOOM

It is Othello's tragedy, but Iago's play. I do not mean that Iago runs off with it, or that Othello's is not a great role. Iago is a dramatist who takes over his fellow characters and plots them into the play that he desires to stage. He is a theatrical improviser, making his plot up as he goes along: He imagines passions for others, and even proposes emotions for himself, which to some degree he subsequently feels. His genius is not as comprehensive as Falstaff's or as Hamlet's, and he lacks the icy joy of Edmund, the brilliant villain of *King Lear*. But his intellect is extraordinary: amazingly quick, endlessly resourceful. Iago is the master psychologist in all of Shakespeare, expert at manipulating everyone else in the play. His pride and analytical interest in his own technique make him also the forerunner of theatrical criticism: as he says, "For I am nothing if not critical."

Montaigne may have taught Shakespeare skepticism, but Shakespeare invented modern nihilism: Hamlet, Iago, Edmund, and Macbeth are its pioneers, direct ancestors of Dostoevsky's Svidrigailov and Stavrogin, and before that, of Milton's Satan in *Paradise Lost,* who is particularly indebted to the diabolical Iago. One useful path into the enigma of Iago's consciousness is provided by the Miltonic "Sense of Injured Merit" that the hero-villain of *Paradise Lost* suffers when he is passed over for Christ, as it were. Coleridge wrote of Iago's "motiveless malignity," but Iago's sense of injured merit is more than motive enough. *The Tragedy of Othello, the Moor of Venice* scarcely can be understood without foregrounding Iago's initial outrage, the permanent wound to his self-regard that was constituted by Othello's rejection of his merit. As the Moor's "ancient" or ensign, Iago bears his captain-general's standard in battle and is professionally pledged to die rather than to allow Othello's colors to be captured. The critic Harold C. Goddard wisely noted that Iago is the spirit of war incarnate, a "moral pyromaniac," who sets the blaze of battle to everyone and to everything. Iago is always at war, which must be why Othello passed over this loyal and courageous fighter and chose Cassio instead as his second-in-command, though Cassio is dismissed by the furious Iago as "a great arithmetician . . . that never set a squadron in the field." Cassio knows the difference between peace and war, a difference that Iago is incapable of knowing. It is the difference that Othello enforces in one magnificent, monosyllabic line that ends a street battle and that confirms Othello in the greatness from which he is soon to fall: "Keep up your bright swords, for the dew will rust them."

The drama begins with Iago affirming truly that he hates the Moor, but the foregrounded implication is that for years he has loved and indeed worshipped Othello, who to Iago would have seemed the god of war incarnate. Iago's nihilistic outcry, "I am not what I am," ensues from a tremendous ontological loss that precedes the start of the play. Iago's predicament is as theological as that of his involuntary disciple, Milton's Satan. You recognize a supreme being, whether your general or your God, as your source of reality, your assured sense of your own value. When you are passed over for another, you become another in the line of Cain, though Iago surpasses the biblical Cain, and Milton's Satan as well. Satan is driven to subvert God's creation, Adam and Eve, but Iago accomplishes the degradation of his war god by reducing Othello to an incoherent murderer. In the metaphysical terms of Melville's *Moby-Dick,* Iago becomes an Ahab who hunts his White Whale in Othello. If Othello was everything and rejected his true servant, Iago, then Iago must seek revenge lest he become nothing at all: "I am not what I am." St. Paul had written, "By the grace of God I am what I am," but what if the grace had been withdrawn?

The negative genius of Iago is fearsome but altogether unquestionable. His sense of injured merit draws from his amazing talents, which he could not have known he possessed and which dazzle him almost as much as they startle us. So awesome a cognitive negativity is as rare in literature as in life. William Hazlitt's superbly equivocal tribute to Iago is not likely to be bettered:

> Our 'Ancient' is a philosopher, who fancies that a lie that kills has more point in it than an alliteration or an antithesis; who thinks a fatal experiment on the peace of a family a better thing

> than watching the palpitations in the heart of a flea in an air-pump; who plots the ruin of his friends as an exercise for his understanding, and stabs men in the dark to prevent *ennui*.

Iago's zest, his energy in evil, has its dangerous aesthetic appeal, and enthralls us as audience even as we are appalled. Shakespeare, who invented the human as we now understand it, did not spare us Iago, the sublime of human negativity. ✤

Biography of William Shakespeare

Few events in the life of William Shakespeare are supported by reliable evidence, and many incidents recorded by commentators of the last four centuries are either conjectural or apocryphal.

William Shakespeare was born in Stratford-upon-Avon on April 22 or 23, 1564, the son of Mary Arden and John Shakespeare, a tradesman. His very early education was in the hands of a tutor, for his parents were probably illiterate. At age seven he entered the Free School in Stratford, where he learned the "small Latin and less Greek" attributed to him by Ben Jonson. When not in school Shakespeare may have gone to the popular Stratford fairs and to the dramas and mystery plays performed by traveling actors.

When Shakespeare was about thirteen his father removed him from school and apprenticed him to a butcher, although it is not known how long he remained in this occupation. When he was eighteen he married Anne Hathaway; their first child, Susanna, was born six months later. A pair of twins, Hamnet and Judith, were born in February 1585. About this time Shakespeare was caught poaching deer on the estate of Sir Thomas Lucy of Charlecot; Lucy's prosecution is said to have inspired Shakespeare to write his earliest literary work, a satire on his opponent. Shakespeare was convicted of poaching and forced to leave Stratford. He withdrew to London, leaving his family behind. He soon attached himself to the stage, initially in a menial capacity (as tender of playgoers' horses, according to one tradition), then as prompter's attendant. When the poaching furor subsided, Shakespeare returned to Stratford to join one of the many bands of itinerant actors. In the next five years he gained what little theater training he received.

By 1592 Shakespeare was a recognized actor, and in that year he wrote and produced his first play, *Henry VI, Part One.* Its success impelled Shakespeare soon afterward to write the second and third parts of *Henry VI.* (Many early and modern critics believed that *Love's Labour's Lost* preceded these histories as Shakespeare's earliest play, but the majority of modern scholars discount this theory.) Shakespeare's popularity provoked the jealousy of Robert Greene, as recorded in his posthumous *Groats-worth of Wit* (1592).

In 1593 Shakespeare published *Venus and Adonis,* a long poem based upon Ovid (or perhaps upon Arthur Golding's translation of Ovid's *Metamorphoses*). It was dedicated to the young earl of Southampton, but perhaps without permission—a possible indication that Shakespeare was trying to gain the nobleman's patronage. However, the dedicatory address to Southampton in the poem *The Rape of Lucrece* (1594) reveals Shakespeare to have been on good terms with him. Many plays—such as *Titus Andronicus, The Comedy of Errors,* and *Romeo and Juliet*—were produced over the next several years, most performed by Shakespeare's troupe, the Lord Chamberlain's Company. In December 1594 Shakespeare acted in a comedy (of unknown authorship) before Queen Elizabeth; many other royal performances followed in the next decade.

In August 1596 Shakespeare's son, Hamnet, died. Early the next year Shakespeare bought a home, New Place, in the center of Stratford; he is said to have planted a mulberry tree in the backyard with his own hands. Shakespeare's relative prosperity is indicated by his purchasing more than a hundred acres of farmland in 1602, a cottage near his estate later that year, and a half-interest in the tithes of some local villages in 1605.

In September 1598 Shakespeare began his friendship with the then unknown Ben Jonson when producing his play *Every Man in His Humour.* The next year the publisher William Jaggard affixed Shakespeare's name, without his permission, to a curious medley of poems under the title *The Passionate Pilgrim;* the majority of the poems were not by Shakespeare. Two of his sonnets, however, appeared in this collection, although the 154 sonnets, with their mysterious dedication to "Mr. W. H.," were not published as a group until 1609. Also in 1599 the Globe Theatre was built in Southwark (an area of London), and Shakespeare's company began acting there. Many of his greatest plays—*Troilus and Cressida, King Lear, Othello, Macbeth*—were performed in the Globe before its destruction by fire in 1613.

The death in 1603 of Queen Elizabeth, the last of the Tudors, and the accession of James I, from the Stuart dynasty of Scotland, created anxiety throughout England. Shakespeare's fortunes, however, were unaffected, as the new monarch extended the license of Shakespeare's company to perform at the Globe. James I saw a performance of *Othello* at the court in November 1604. In October 1605 Shakespeare's company performed before the Mayor and Corporation of Oxford.

The last five years of Shakespeare's life seem void of incident; he had retired from the stage by 1613. Among the few known incidents is Shakespeare's involvement in a heated and lengthy dispute about the enclosure of common-fields around Stratford. He died on April 23, 1616, and was buried in the Church of St. Mary's in Stratford. A monument was later erected to him in the Poets' Corner of Westminster Abbey.

Numerous corrupt quarto editions of Shakespeare's plays were published during his lifetime. These editions, based either on manuscripts, promptbooks, or sometimes merely actors' recollections of the plays, were meant to capitalize on Shakespeare's renown. Other plays, now deemed wholly or largely spurious—*Edward III, The Yorkshire Tragedy, The Two Noble Kinsmen,* and others—were also published under Shakespeare's name during and after his lifetime. Shakespeare's plays were collected in the First Folio of 1623 by John Heminge and Henry Condell. Nine years later the Second Folio was published, and in 1640 Shakespeare's poems were collected. The first standard collected edition was by Nicholas Rowe (1709), followed by the editions of Alexander Pope (1725), Lewis Theobald (1733), Samuel Johnson (1765), Edmond Malone (1790), and many others.

Shakespeare's plays are now customarily divided into the following categories (probable dates of writing are given in brackets): comedies (*The Comedy of Errors* [1590], *The Taming of the Shrew* [1592], *The Two Gentlemen of Verona* [1592–93], *A Midsummer Night's Dream* [1595], *Love's Labour's Lost* [1595], *The Merchant of Venice* [1596–98], *As You Like It* [1597], *The Merry Wives of Windsor* [1597], *Much Ado About Nothing* [1598–99], *Twelfth Night* [1601], *All's Well That Ends Well* [1603–04], and *Measure for Measure* [1604]); histories

(*Henry VI, Part One* [1590–92], *Henry VI, Parts Two and Three* [1590–92], *Richard III* [1591], *King John* [1591–98], *Richard II* [1595], *Henry IV, Part One* [1597], *Henry IV, Part Two* [1597], *Henry V* [1599], and *Henry VIII* [1613]); tragedies (*Titus Andronicus* [1590], *Romeo and Juliet* [1595], *Julius Caesar* [1599], *Hamlet* [1599–1601], *Troilus and Cressida* [1602], *Othello* [1602–04], *King Lear* [1604–05], *Macbeth* [1606], *Timon of Athens* [1607], *Antony and Cleopatra* [1606–07], and *Coriolanus* [1608]); and romances (*Pericles, Prince of Tyre* [1606–08], *Cymbeline* [1609–10], *The Winter's Tale* [1610–11], and *The Tempest* [1611]). However, Shakespeare willfully defied the canons of classical drama by mingling comedy, tragedy, and history, so that in some cases classification is debatable or arbitrary.

Shakespeare's reputation, while subject to many fluctuations, was firmly established by the eighteenth century. Samuel Johnson remarked: "Perhaps it would not be easy to find any authour, except Homer, who invented so much as Shakespeare, who so much advanced the studies which he cultivated, who effused so much novelty upon his age or country. The form, the characters, the language, and the shows of the English drama are his." Early in the nineteenth century Samuel Taylor Coleridge declared: "The Englishman who without reverence, a proud and affectionate reverence, can utter the name of William Shakespeare, stands disqualified for the office of critic. . . . Great as was the genius of Shakespeare, his judgment was at least equal to it."

A curious controversy developed in the middle of the nineteenth century in regard to the authorship of Shakespeare's plays, some contending that Sir Francis Bacon was the actual author of the plays, others (including Mark Twain) advancing the claims of the earl of Oxford. None of these attempts has succeeded in persuading the majority of scholars that Shakespeare himself is not the author of the plays attributed to him.

In recent years many landmark editions of Shakespeare, with increasingly accurate texts and astute critical commentary, have emerged. These include *The Arden Shakespeare* (1951–), *The Oxford Shakespeare* (1982–), and *The New Cambridge*

Shakespeare (1984–). Such critics as T. S. Eliot, G. Wilson Knight, Northrop Frye, W. H. Auden, and many others have continued to elucidate Shakespeare, his work, and his times, and he remains the most written-about author in the history of English literature. ✣

Thematic and Structural Analysis

Shakespeare's *Othello* recounts the tragic consequences of hatred, jealousy, revenge, and exploited and misplaced trust. **Act I, scene 1** opens in Venice with Iago telling Roderigo, a gentleman of Venice, about his jealousy and hatred of Cassio, a soldier who has recently been promoted to lieutenant. Iago, who himself aspired to the position, spitefully criticizes Cassio's military prowess, while complaining that he, hassled by "debitor and creditor," must remain "his Moorship's ancient"—his ensign or standard-bearer. It soon becomes clear, however, that "his Moorship," the Venetian general Othello (who remains unnamed throughout the scene) is the primary object of Iago's hate. While Iago pretends to be a steadfast follower, he loathes Othello and is primarily concerned with his own well-being, rather than his duty. He tells Roderigo that his false show of loyalty and honesty provides the ideal cloak for machinations to advance his own agenda: "In following him, I follow but myself . . . not I for love and duty, / But seeming so, for my peculiar end. . . ."

Iago begins to plot his revenge on Othello and Cassio and enlists Roderigo as his accomplice. Iago tells Roderigo that "the Moor" has married the daughter of Brabantio, a Venetian senator, and convinces him to cause a scandal in front of Brabantio's house. When first roused, Brabantio orders Roderigo, who seems to be an admirer of the senator's daughter, to leave. However, he then listens, horrified, as the pair reveals that his daughter, Desdemona, has secretly married Othello. The language Iago and Roderigo use to incite the senator's anger is clearly prejudiced; they refer to Othello as "an old black ram," a "Barbary horse," and a "lascivious Moor." Iago then leaves Roderigo to accompany Brabantio in search of his daughter and the Moor.

The play then shifts abruptly from the opening mystery of Iago's hatred and revenge to our first glimpse of the Moor (**I.2**). Iago stands at Othello's side, warning Othello, who we learn is a successful military officer and of noble birth, about

Brabantio's anger. Cassio enters with an urgent message about the ongoing conflict over Cyprus. While Othello notifies his household of his imminent departure to the island, Iago begins to tell Cassio of Othello's marriage but is interrupted when Othello returns. At the same time, a furious Brabantio arrives, followed by Roderigo and others, and accuses Othello of robbing him of his daughter. They all go off to the duke of Venice to settle the matter.

In contrast to the brevity of scene 2, **Act I, scene 3** is lengthy and includes a series of confrontations, accusations, and declarations. It begins with the duke and his senators discussing the threat of a Turkish attack on Cyprus. When Othello arrives, the duke welcomes him and orders him to leave for Cyprus. Brabantio's presence, however, interrupts the duke's thoughts, allowing the senator to begin his accusations against Othello: "She is abused, stol'n from me, and corrupted, / By spells and medicines. . . ." Othello admits that he has married Desdemona but with her complete consent; he did not bewitch her. However, Brabantio's exclamation—that "[t]o fall in love with what she fear'd to look on" goes "[a]gainst all rules of nature"—highlights the real problem: the color of Othello's skin. By marrying a Moor, a black-skinned man, Desdemona has entered into an "unnatural" union.

Brabantio demands that Othello be imprisoned, but the general asks that Desdemona be sent for to prove that he did not enchant her. The duke agrees, and while they await Desdemona, Othello explains that he wooed Desdemona during his visits to Brabantio's house by telling her of his life and its adventures. He assures the assembled men, "She loved me for the dangers I had passed, / And I loved her that she did pity them. This is the only witchcraft I have used." Upon her arrival, Desdemona pays her respects to her father but declares that her duty and love are now Othello's. Although Brabantio ceases his accusations and recognizes Othello as Desdemona's husband, he remains clearly upset. The duke and the others immediately return to matters of state and decide that Othello will leave for Cyprus in the morning. Desdemona asks for and receives permission to accompany him. The duke poignantly comments to Brabantio, "Your son-in-law is far more fair than black," suggesting that all is resolved. However, Brabantio's remarks to Othello hint at a darker future: "Look to her, Moor, if thou has eyes to see: / She has deceived her father, and may thee." Othello's reply is even more foreboding: "My life upon her faith. . . ."

From these ominous words, the scene shifts to the coconspirators, Iago and Roderigo. Roderigo threatens to drown himself out of unrequited love for Desdemona and, when Iago rebukes him, protests that he cannot control his state of mind for "it is not in [his] virtue to amend it." To this Iago replies, "Virtue? a fig! 'Tis in ourselves that we are thus and thus. Our bodies are our gardens, to which our wills are gardeners. . . ." He notes that it is reason alone that keeps "the blood and baseness of our natures" from "conduct[ing] us to most preposterous conclusions." Inciting Roderigo to "come, be a man!" Iago tells him not to give up on Desdemona and to follow the couple to Cyprus, with, of course, an ample supply of money. Urging cooperation, Iago assures that Desdemona will soon tire of Othello and promises his accomplice to help him win her affections. He tells Roderigo that his cuckolding Othello will be ample vengeance for both men. Roderigo vows to sell his land and exits, leaving Iago alone.

In a soliloquy, Iago makes it clear that he is using Roderigo for his money and divulges the cause of his hatred for Othello—a rumor that Othello has had an affair with his wife: "I hate the Moor; / And it is thought abroad that 'twixt my sheets / H'as done my office." Iago outlines his strategy, a double plot that will harm Cassio and Othello by casting doubt on Desdemona's fidelity. He emphasizes that Othello's "free and open nature / That thinks men honest that but seem so" will allow Iago to exact his revenge easily. Iago exits, exclaiming, "Hell and night / Must bring this monstrous birth to the world's light."

Act II, scene 1 opens in Cyprus at the seaport, where Cassio, Montano, the governor of Cyprus, and other gentlemen await the arrival of Othello. There is a distinct break in time between Acts I and II, the only such break in the play. Little time appears to elapse between the acts that follow; in fact, the remainder of the play's action seems to take place in only a few days. At the port we learn that a storm has badly damaged the

Turkish fleet. The first ship to arrive, however, is carrying Iago and Desdemona, who is in his care. Cassio welcomes them and informs Desdemona that Othello's ship is not yet in port. While on the quay, Iago, his wife Emilia, and Desdemona talk lightly of women, those who are fair, dark, light-headed, or witty. In an aside, Iago is pleased to see Cassio treat Desdemona so attentively, believing that the lieutenant's gallant conduct will facilitate his plot. When Othello's ship finally arrives, the general greets Desdemona warmly and announces that the "wars are done; the Turks are drowned." Then all leave for the castle except Iago and Roderigo, who remain behind to discuss their conspiracy.

Iago declares that Cassio loves Desdemona and promises that she will succumb quickly to his attentions, thus convincing Roderigo to pick a fight with the lieutenant during his watch that evening. After Roderigo departs, Iago, in his closing soliloquy, reiterates his hatred of Othello and his desire to avenge the general's alleged cuckoldry:

> And nothing can or shall content my soul
> Till I am evened with him, wife for wife;
> Or failing so, yet that I put the Moor
> At least into a jealousy so strong
> That judgement cannot cure.

Iago plans to drive Othello to madness through jealousy by framing Cassio and Desdemona for adultery, while reaping thanks and rewards from Othello for his efforts.

The following scene is brief and transitional (**II.2**): A herald proclaims that all should celebrate Othello's victory over the Turks and his marriage. **Act II, scene 3**, however, is long and involved. It opens with Othello assigning Cassio to the watch, after which Iago gets the on-duty Cassio drunk in the presence of Montano and other gentlemen, to whom he reveals his doubts about Cassio's character and dependability. Roderigo, on Iago's instructions, provokes Cassio, who retaliates by starting a fight in which Montano is wounded. Iago pretends to intercede just as Othello arrives. Montano leaves all the explaining to Iago, who shrewdly feigns humility and reticence in accusing Cassio. Othello mistakenly interprets this as a product of Iago's reputed honor and, as a result, discharges Cassio from service.

Desdemona then enters the scene and all depart, leaving Iago talking to a dejected Cassio, who says that he has been gravely wounded, not in body, but in image: "I have lost my reputation! I have lost the immortal part of myself and what remains is bestial." Iago, perhaps ironically and certainly hypocritically, reassures him, "Reputation is an idle and most false imposition; oft got without merit and lost without deserving. You have lost no reputation at all unless you repute yourself such a loser." Cassio then laments his actions and the effects of the alcohol that induced them, wondering "that we should with joy, pleasance, revel, and applause transform ourselves into beasts!" Iago tells Cassio not to be so hard on himself and suggests that he can regain his former standing with Othello if he asks Desdemona to intercede on his behalf.

Thus reassured, Cassio bids Iago good night, leaving him to consider the next phase of his plan, in which his "good" advice will destroy Cassio: "Divinity of hell! When devils will the blackest sins put on, / They do suggest at first with heavenly shows, / As I do now." He will suggest to Othello that Cassio and Desdemona are having an affair and thus "turn [Desdemona's] virtue into pitch, / And out of her own goodness make the net / that shall enmesh them all." Iago is then briefly interrupted by Roderigo, who complains that he has no more money and must return to Venice. Iago counsels patience—"What wound did ever heal but by degrees"—and Roderigo exits. Iago then embellishes his scheme further, deciding to include his wife and to put his plot in motion immediately.

In Acts I and II, Othello, in spite of the domestic conflict he creates, has been depicted as a noble and loyal general, a just, rational man who is successful in his endeavors. In Act III, however, Othello begins his fall from reasoned judgment to irrational obsession. **Act III, scene 1** begins innocently enough with Cassio accompanied by musicians and a clown. Iago enters and greets Cassio, who tells him that he is waiting for Emilia in the hopes that she will arrange a meeting with Desdemona. Emilia agrees and assures Cassio that Desdemona is defending him to Othello. The scene that follows is extremely brief; Othello sends Iago off with orders to his ships and commands the ensign to report back to him (**III.2**).

A quick conversation between Desdemona and Cassio, with Emilia in attendance, opens **Act III, scene 3**. Just as Desdemona agrees to intercede on Cassio's behalf, Othello and Iago are seen approaching. Cassio slips away, and Iago, of course, points out the lieutenant's uneasy departure to Othello. Desdemona tries to discuss Cassio's case with her husband, but since his mind is on other matters, Othello asks her to leave him for the moment, promising to talk to Cassio later.

Alone with Othello, Iago continues to discuss Cassio and manipulates the conversation to cause the general to question Cassio's honesty, beginning by asking if Cassio knew of Othello's courtship of Desdemona. As the conversation continues, Iago spikes his replies to Othello's questions with so many innuendos and deliberate hesitations that Othello, frustrated and convinced that Iago is concealing information, insists that he speak candidly. Othello praises Iago as "full of love and honesty" as the ensign casts doubts on Cassio's character and stresses, ironically, the importance of appearances ("Men should be what they seem. . . .") and reputation ("Good name in man and woman. . . / Is the immediate jewel of their souls."). Cunningly, Iago warns Othello against jealousy, the "green-eyed monster." Othello is still in possession of his judgment and does not blindly accept Iago's aspersions: ". . . No, Iago, I'll see before I doubt. . . ."

Iago, however, does not let up and suggests that Othello observe Desdemona in Cassio's presence. He shrewdly appeals to Othello's alleged lack of experience with Venetian women, implying that not only is Othello unskilled in personal matters but also that these women hide a great deal from their husbands. As Othello's doubts begin to take hold, Iago pushes even further by reminding Othello that Desdemona deceived her father to marry him. Though Othello claims, "I do not but think Desdemona honest," he asks Iago to keep him informed and to have Emilia watch her. As Iago is leaving, Othello ponders, "Why did I marry? This honest creature doubtless / Sees and knows more, much more, than he unfolds." Othello is thus beginning to doubt Desdemona, while still believing in Iago's reputed honesty. Othello's poignant soliloquy, in which he reveals his doubts about himself—the color of his skin, his unrefined speech, his age—begins by referring to Iago's "exceeding honesty" and ends by questioning Desdemona's virtue.

Desdemona and Emilia enter the scene, breaking the tension that pervades the atmosphere, and call Othello to dinner. As they leave, Desdemona accidentally drops her handkerchief, the first gift she received from Othello. It seems a small detail until Emilia, who has picked up the handkerchief, gives it to her husband. Iago, who has repeatedly asked Emilia to steal the token, cannot believe his good luck, for the handkerchief will allow him to confirm the poisonous doubts he has planted in Othello's mind.

Othello now returns and resumes his earlier discussion with Iago. A change in Othello has taken place as he himself acknowledges: ". . . O now for ever / Farewell the tranquil mind! farewell content!" Extremely frustrated by the jealousy that has begun to gnaw at him, Othello turns on Iago, calls him a villain, and insists that he provide "ocular proof" of his accusations. Again Iago hesitates, thus increasing Othello's agitation. When Othello insists that he be direct, Iago finally agrees to provide evidence: "[I]f imputation and strong circumstances / Which lead directly to the door of truth / Will give you satisfaction, you may have't." Iago tells Othello that as Cassio slept, the lieutenant uttered, "Sweet Desdemona, / Let us be wary, let us hide our loves!" and that he saw Cassio wipe his beard with Desdemona's handkerchief. Here Iago kneels and begs Othello to command him. Othello has fallen into the well-laid trap and, caught in an irrational frenzy of revenge, orders that Cassio die within three days. By the end of the scene, Iago has accomplished several of his goals: Cassio is ruined, Desdemona is suspected of infidelity, and Iago is appointed Othello's lieutenant. This last success may be Iago's sweetest, for he has not simply retained his image as an honest servant but has risen in rank, influence, and power precisely because of his dishonesty. He tells Othello, "I am your own forever."

Act III, scene 4 begins with a genial play on words between the clown and Desdemona, who asks where to find Cassio. When Emilia asks if Othello is jealous, Desdemona assures her that he is not. Desdemona is still planning to intercede on Cassio's behalf with Othello, who by now suspects her of adultery. The entrance of Othello, greatly agitated, interrupts Desdemona's conversation with the clown. When Desdemona unwittingly brings up the subject of Cassio, Othello asks for her handkerchief. When she tells him she does not have it with her, Othello chastises her and recounts, or perhaps invents, the handkerchief's history, importance, and magic. But Desdemona insists on discussing Cassio's dilemma, while Othello demands to know the handkerchief's whereabouts. Frustrated by the conversation, Othello leaves. Emilia, now certain that Othello is jealous, comments, "Tis not a year or two shows us a man. / They are all but stomachs, and we all but food; / They eat us hungerly, and when they are full, / They belch us."

Iago and Cassio then join Desdemona and Emilia. Cassio asks once again for Desdemona's assistance. Desdemona and Emilia discuss Othello's unusual state of frustration, wondering what "[h]ath puddled his spirit." Emilia is hopeful that matters of state are provoking his agitation rather than unfounded jealousy—which is a "monster, / Begat upon itself, born on itself." When the two women exit, Cassio is joined by Bianca, his courtesan. Cassio explains his recent absences to Bianca and gives her Desdemona's handkerchief. When he asks her to copy its embroidery, she inquires about its former owner. Cassio responds that he knows nothing, since he only recently found it in his sleeping quarters. Act III ends as the two part, with the handkerchief now in circulation as Iago desired.

As **Act IV, scene 1** begins, Iago and Othello are in the middle of a conversation. When Iago once again mentions Desdemona's handkerchief, saying that it was hers to give away, Othello equates the handkerchief with Desdemona's honor, wondering if that too can be awarded at will. Iago works Othello into such a frenzy that the general collapses on the floor in a trance. Iago delights in Othello's loss of physical and mental control: "Work on, my medicine, work! Thus credulous fools are caught, / And many worthy and chaste dames, even thus, / All guiltless, meet reproach. . . ."

When Cassio enters the scene and inquires about Othello, Iago replies that Othello is having an epileptic attack, and Cassio momentarily withdraws. As Othello comes to his senses, he laments that a cuckold is "a monster and a beast," to which Iago replies, "There's many a beast then in a populous city, / And many a civil monster." Iago then reports that Cassio is close by. Othello cannot contain himself, but Iago suggests that he be patient and let Cassio confirm his own treachery. He has Othello step out of view to eavesdrop on Iago's conversation with Cassio, who returns as Othello withdraws. Iago's plan is to have Cassio talk of Bianca but let Othello think that Cassio is speaking of Desdemona. The plot proceeds as planned until Bianca unexpectedly enters. But Iago is able to turn even her words against Cassio. Bianca chides him for having given her the handkerchief of another woman and leaves in a huff. Iago then encourages Cassio to run after her to seek forgiveness. In the meantime, Othello can no longer control his anger and reiterates his intention to murder Cassio. To incense Othello further, Iago mentions the handkerchief again, thus provoking Othello to contemplate murdering Desdemona as well. Othello asks Iago to get him some poison for this purpose, but Iago now is so confident of his control over Othello that he even suggests how Othello should kill her: "Do it not with poison. Strangle her in her bed, even / the bed she hath contaminated."

As Othello agrees to the plan ("The justice of it pleases"), Desdemona arrives with a kinsman, Lodovico, who brings Othello a letter from the duke. The exchange between Othello and Lodovico, cordial and appropriate for their station and purpose, contrasts with that between Othello and Desdemona, in which Othello betrays his obsessive state of mind. Reading the letter, Othello learns that he is to return to Venice However, even as he reads, his thoughts and words are repeatedly directed to Desdemona, whom he berates, insults, and finally strikes. Lodovico reacts with obvious surprise and remarks that such behavior "would not be believed in Venice." To avoid further confrontation, Desdemona withdraws. As she does, Othello reveals that the letter instructs Cassio to replace Othello in Cyprus. The coincidence is too great for Othello, and he exits. As the scene ends, Lodovico remains with Iago, who takes advantage of Othello's lamentable behavior to discredit the once-temperate and just general in front of Lodovico.

While the second scenes of Acts I, II, and III were brief and transitional, **Act IV, scene 2** maintains the tension and level of complexity that opened the act. First Othello interrogates Emilia, who defends Desdemona's honor. Then, he confronts Desdemona, calling her a "whore" and a "weed, / Who art so lovely fair, and smell'st so sweet," suggesting that her pleasing appearance conceals her true character. After he leaves, Desdemona discusses the attack with Emilia and Iago, who, of course, pretends not to understand. Emilia comes very close to the truth when she speculates that someone trying to advance in office has planned such slander, also reminding Iago that he falsely suspected her of being involved with Othello. Iago ignores her so that he can focus on Desdemona, whom he advises to be patient. When the two women leave, Roderigo enters, frustrated and complaining that Iago has not kept his promise to win Desdemona for him. Once again Iago strings him along and changes the subject, informing Roderigo that Othello will be leaving and that Cassio will take his place. In order to prevent Othello's departure, and so Desdemona's, Roderigo should make Cassio "uncapable of Othello's place—knocking out his brains." They plan to attack him that evening, and Iago promises to act as Roderigo's second. The scene ends as they leave to discuss their plans further.

At the beginning of **Act IV, scene 3**, Othello appears calmer. Emilia and Desdemona comment on this as Desdemona prepares for bed. Desdemona tells Emilia about the tragic death of one of her mother's servants, abandoned by a lover who "proved mad." She sings the song "Willow," which the maid died singing. Othello has told her to send Emilia away for the evening, but before she does, Desdemona asks Emilia if there really are women who deceive their husbands. A seemingly wise Emilia assures her that there are, despite Desdemona's pledges that she would be incapable of such behavior. Interestingly, Emilia notes that it is "their husbands' faults / If wives do fall." She wonders, "And have we not affections, / Desires for sport, and frailty, as men have? / Then let them use us well; else let them know, / The ills we do, their wills instruct us so." The act closes as Desdemona bids her good night.

Act V, like Act IV, starts with a conversation already in progress, once again emphasizing a continuation of action and intensity (**V.1**). Iago and Roderigo are preparing to attack Cassio. Iago steps away as Cassio enters the scene and, in an aside, observes that both men must die. He has been keeping the gold and jewels that Roderigo has given him as gifts for Desdemona and dreads having to return them. Cassio's survival will also jeopardize Iago: "He hath a daily beauty in his life / That make me ugly; and besides, the Moor / May unfold me to him. . . ." Roderigo takes a stab at Cassio, who draws his sword and wounds Roderigo. From his hiding place, Iago wounds Cassio—perhaps disabling him—and withdraws.

The shouts of Cassio attract Othello's attention; believing that Iago has killed Cassio, Othello praises his ensign's loyalty and honesty and heads towards Desdemona's room to carry out his part. In the meantime, Lodovico and Gratiano, another relative of Desdemona, alerted by the shouts, arrive on the scene and are joined by Iago. Iago takes advantage of the confusion to stab and kill Roderigo. Bianca then enters and becomes distraught when she sees the wounded Cassio, whom the gentlemen bear off in a chair. Emilia comes in and hears of the attack from Iago. He explains away the situation as the result of carousing and tries to implicate Bianca, thus shifting the attention, once again, away from himself. As the scene ends, Iago now knows that the evening's events will determine his future: "This is the night / That either makes me or fordoes me quite."

The play now shifts to Desdemona's bedroom (**V.2**), where she is asleep when Othello enters. He regards his sleeping wife and, in agony, reiterates the necessity of killing her to prevent her from "betray[ing] more men" but suggests that murdering her is the only way to restore his love and her virtue: "If I quench thee . . . I can thy former light restore." Othello then kisses Desdemona and, when she awakes, tells her to pray, because he "would not kill [her] soul." Finally, Othello accuses her of having given both her handkerchief and her favors to Cassio. Othello does not listen to her denials, clinging to the handkerchief as evidence and refusing her request to call Cassio to confirm her story. Even though Desdemona insists on her innocence and begs for mercy, Othello sticks to his plan. As he chokes her, Desdemona cries out. Emilia hears the voices and tries to enter the room; when she finally gets the door open, she rushes to the dying Desdemona's aid but is too late. Enraged by Desdemona's death, Emilia launches a verbal attack against Othello that is interrupted only when Othello states that it was her husband, Iago, who revealed Desdemona's infidelity to him. Emilia realizes that her husband has fabricated the plot and cries for help.

When Iago appears accompanied by Montano and Gratiano, Emilia challenges Iago: "You told a lie, an odious, damned lie!" While Othello explains why he has murdered his wife, we learn from Gratiano that Brabantio has died of grief over his daughter's marriage. Othello mentions the handkerchief, triggering an even stronger reaction in Emilia, for she now completely understands the lengths to which Iago has gone in his treachery. She starts to accuse him, and Iago draws his sword against her. They exchange harsh words, which cause Othello to come to his senses. He attacks Iago, but Iago stabs his wife and flees, pursued by Montano and Gratiano. Othello, now finally in a state of clarity but racked by the pain of his actions, listens to Emilia's final accusation as she dies.

Othello searches for and finds a special sword in the room. Looking at the weapon, he sorrowfully remembers his past successes and laments, "But O vain boast! / Who can control his fate? 'Tis not so now." As he sadly contemplates his wife's dead body, the gentlemen return with the captured Iago. Othello wounds him with his sword but is stopped from harming him further by the men. They question him about the plot with Iago to kill Cassio. Othello admits his part in the plan and begs the forgiveness of Cassio. Letters have been found on Roderigo's dead body implicating Iago as author of the conspiracy, and Cassio explains to Othello how Desdemona's handkerchief came into his possession. Lodovico announces that, because of his actions, Othello will be removed from power and be replaced by Cassio. He also states that Iago will face trial, torture, and imprisonment.

Othello is to return for trial as well, but he stops to remind them all of his service to the state:

> Speak of me as I am. Nothing extenuate,
> Nor set down in malice. Then you must speak
> Of one that loved not wisely, but too well;
> Of one not easily jealous, but being wrought,
> Perplexed in the extreme; of one whose hand,
> Like the base Judean, threw a pearl away
> Richer than all his tribe. . . .

When he finishes, he stabs himself, falls on Desdemona's bed, and dies, crying out: "I kissed thee ere I killed thee, no way but this, / Killing myself, to die upon a kiss." The play ends with Lodovico berating Iago and urging Montano to punish the villain severely, while Lodovico himself returns to Venice, where he will "[t]his heavy act with heavy heart relate." ✤

—*Elizabeth Beaudin*
Yale University

List of Characters

Othello is a successful Venetian general of noble birth. However, as a Moor, his ethnicity, dark skin, and non-Christian birth set him apart. When Othello secretly marries Desdemona, daughter of a Venetian senator, he oversteps invisible boundaries. In spite of his distinguished military record, his marriage to a white Venetian woman is considered an unnatural alliance; it is alleged that the blackness of his skin is only a thin cover for the blackness of his unbaptized heathen soul. Over the course of the play, Iago's machinations lead him to behave like the "savage" he is reputed to be. As he becomes embroiled in the plot laid for his downfall, his reason and judgment give way to obsessive rage. Ironically it is Othello's judgment that allows Iago to manipulate him; Othello is a trusting man who believes that people are what they seem, thus believing in Iago because he appears to be honest and loyal. Thinking that his wife, Desdemona, has had an affair with his lieutenant, Cassio, Othello strangles her, only to kill himself after realizing that he was tricked by his trusted servant.

Iago is Othello's "ancient," his ensign or standard-bearer. Iago plots to advance himself and to destroy Othello and Cassio by suggesting to Othello that Cassio and Desdemona are having an affair and thereby driving Othello to murder. While Iago is Othello's inferior in military rank and experience, he exceeds his general is his ability to calculate and maintain control of his plan. That others repeatedly refer to Iago as "honest" is both ironic and accurate: While Iago uses his reputation for honesty and loyalty as a sham to manipulate Othello, he is always honest to himself—to his goals of revenge and self-advancement and to his motivations of jealousy throughout the web of lies he spins. While Iago's guilt is revealed by his wife, Emilia, whom he murders in the play's final scene, he ultimately succeeds in his plan to ruin Othello.

Desdemona is the virtuous daughter of Brabantio, a Venetian senator. She marries Othello, who strangles her, believing her guilty of adultery with Cassio. While Desdemona is often thought of as a passive child-bride with little personality, she does exhibit her own will. By marrying Othello, who is outside the circle of acceptable suitors, without her father's permission, Desdemona flouts parental authority and social convention. Ironically, this independence, which indicates the strength of her love for Othello, becomes her undoing. Iago uses Desdemona's deception of her father to cause Othello to doubt his wife's virtue and honesty and to kill her.

Cassio is Othello's recently promoted lieutenant. Although his character is not well developed, Cassio is a key figure in Iago's plot. Iago's jealousy of Cassio—he desired the post of lieutenant—leads Iago to include Cassio in his revenge against Othello. The play's action revolves around Iago's attempts to destroy Cassio by creating a fictitious and illicit relation between him and Desdemona. While Iago succeeds in wounding and perhaps crippling Cassio, the lieutenant survives to take over Othello's post at the end of the play.

Emilia is Iago's wife and maid-servant to Desdemona. Despite her devotion to Desdemona, she unknowingly helps Iago's plans by securing Desdemona's handkerchief, which becomes Iago's primary piece of evidence "proving" Desdemona and Cassio's "affair." In the final scenes, Emilia defends Desdemona's innocence to Othello and reveals Iago's infamy, only to be stabbed by her husband. In contrast to Desdemona, Emilia is a worldly woman who speaks candidly about adultery and sexual relations.

Roderigo is a gentleman of Venice whom Iago enlists in his revenge. Iago promises the gullible Roderigo that he will arrange an assignation with Desdemona, whom Roderigo loves. But Iago, troubled with financial problems, exploits Roderigo for his wealth and uses him as a foil in the conspiracy against Cassio. Iago eventually kills Roderigo to cover his tracks and to avoid returning gold and jewels he has embezzled.

Bianca is Cassio's courtesan. In his conspiracy against Cassio, Iago stages a conversation with Cassio about Bianca, allowing Othello to overhear it and believe they are discussing Desdemona. At the end of the play, Iago tries to implicate Bianca in Cassio's death.

Brabantio is a Venetian senator and the father of Desdemona. Personifying the discrimination against Othello, Brabantio is deeply upset at his daughter's marriage to "the Moor." At the end of the play, we learn that he died because of his grief about the union.

The *duke of Venice* sends Othello to Cyprus on a military mission. However, he first acts as intermediary between Brabantio and Othello when the senator accuses Othello of using witchcraft to enchant Desdemona into marrying him.

Lodovico, a relative of Desdemona, is a messenger from Venice. He witnesses the final downfall of Othello and Iago.

Montano and *Gratiano* are respectively the governor of Cyprus and a relative of Desdemona. Along with Lodovico, these nobles witness the end of life, power, and conspiracy in the play's final act. ✣

Critical Views

THOMAS RYMER ON THE IMPLAUSIBLE CHARACTERS IN *OTHELLO*

[Thomas Rymer (1641–1713) was a pioneering British critic who wrote *The Tragedies of the Last Age* (1678) and *A Short View of Tragedy* (1692), from which the following extract is taken. Here, Rymer—who, as a defender of the "ancients" (the Greek and Latin dramatists) against the "moderns," or contemporary writers—takes a harsh view of *Othello,* finding the characters implausible and unrealistic.]

The *Characters* or Manners, which are the second part in a Tragedy, are not less unnatural and improper, than the Fable was improbable and absurd.

Othello is made a Venetian General. We see nothing done by him, nor related concerning him, that comports with the condition of a General, or, indeed, of a Man, unless the killing himself, to avoid a death the Law was about to inflict upon him. When his Jealousy had wrought him up to a resolution of's taking revenge for the suppos'd injury, He sets *Jago* to the fighting part, to kill *Cassio;* And chuses himself to murder the silly Woman his Wife, that was like to make no resistance.

His Love and his Jealousie are no part of a Souldiers Character, unless for Comedy.

But what is most intolerable is *Jago.* He is no Black-amoor Souldier, so we may be sure he should be like other Souldiers of our acquaintance; yet never in Tragedy, nor in Comedy, nor in Nature was a Souldier with his Character; take it in the Authors own words;

> *Em.:* —some Eternal Villain,
> Some busie, and insinuating Rogue,
> Some cogging, couzening Slave, to get some Office.

Horace Describes a Souldier otherwise:

Impiger, iracundus, inexorabilis, acer.

Shakespear knew his Character of *Jago* was inconsistent. In this very Play he pronounces,

If thou dost deliver more or less than Truth,
Thou are no Souldier.—

This he knew, but to entertain the Audience with something new and surprising, against common sense, and Nature, he would pass upon us a close, dissembling, false, insinuating rascal, instead of an open-hearted, frank, plain-dealing Souldier, a character constantly worn by them for some thousands of years in the World.

Tiberius Cæsar had a Poet Arraign'd for his Life: because *Agamemnon* was brought on the Stage by him, with a character unbecoming a Souldier.

Our *Ensigns* and Subalterns, when disgusted by the Captain, throw up their Commissions, bluster, and are bare-fac'd. *Jago*, I hope, is not brought on the Stage, in a Red Coat. I know not what Livery the Venetians wear: but am sure they hold not these conditions to be *alla soldatesca*.

Non sia egli per fare la vendetta con insidie, ma con la spada in mano. *Cinthio*.

Nor is our Poet more discreet in his *Desdemona*, He had chosen a Souldier for his Knave: And a Venetian Lady is to be the Fool.

This Senators Daughter runs away to (a Carriers Inn) the *Sagittary*, with a Black-amoor: is no sooner wedded to him, but the very night she Beds him, is importuning and teizing him for a young smock-fac'd Lieutenant, *Cassio*. And tho' she perceives the *Moor* Jealous of *Cassio*, yet will she not forbear, but still rings *Cassio*, *Cassio* in both his Ears.

Roderigo is the Cully of *Jago*, brought in to be murder'd by *Jago*, that *Jago*'s hands might be the more in Blood, and be yet the more abominable Villain: who without that was too wicked on all Conscience; And had more to answer for, than any Tragedy, or Furies could inflict upon him. So there can be nothing in the *characters,* either for the profit, or to delight an Audience.

—Thomas Rymer, *A Short View of Tragedy* (1692), *The Critical Works of Thomas Rymer,* ed. Curt A. Zimansky (New Haven: Yale University Press, 1956), pp. 134–36

✣

SAMUEL JOHNSON ON THE GREATNESS OF *OTHELLO*

[Samuel Johnson (1709–1784), perhaps the greatest British literary figure of the eighteenth century, was a poet, novelist, critic, and biographer of distinction. In 1765 he wrote a monograph, *Preface to His Edition of Shakespeare,* and in that same year he edited a landmark annotated edition of Shakespeare's works, still highly regarded for the astuteness of its commentary. In this extract, taken from the notes to his edition, Johnson speaks of the greatness of *Othello,* especially in regard to its characters.]

The beauties of this play impress themselves so strongly upon the attention of the reader, that they can draw no aid from critical illustration. The fiery openness of Othello, magnanimous, artless, and credulous, boundless in his confidence, ardent in his affection, inflexible in his resolution, and obdurate in his revenge; the cool malignity of Iago, silent in his resentment, subtle in his designs, and studious at once of his interest and his vengeance; the soft simplicity of Desdemona, confident of merit, and conscious of innocence, her artless perseverance in her suit, and her slowness to suspect that she can be suspected, are such proofs of Shakespeare's skill in human nature, as, I suppose, it is vain to seek in any modern writer. The gradual process which Iago makes in the Moor's conviction, and the circumstances which he employs to inflame him, are so artfully natural, that, though it will perhaps not be said of him as he says of himself, that he is "a man not easily jealous," yet we cannot but pity him when at last we find him "perplexed in the extreme."

There is always danger lest wickedness conjoined with abilities should steal upon esteem, though it misses of approbation; but the character of Iago is so conducted, that he is from the first scene to the last hated and despised.

Even the inferiour characters of this play would be very conspicuous in any other piece, not only for their justness but their strength. Cassio is brave, benevolent, and honest, ruined only by his want of stubbornness to resist an insidious invitation. Rodorigo's suspicious credulity, and impatient submission to the cheats which he sees practised upon him, and which by persuasion he suffers to be repeated, exhibit a strong picture of a weak mind betrayed by unlawful desires, to a false friend; and the virtue of Aemilia is such as we often find, worn loosely, but not cast off, easy to commit small crimes, but quickened and alarmed at atrocious villanies.

The scenes from the beginning to the end are busy, varied by happy interchanges, and regularly promoting the progression of the story; and the narrative in the end, though it tells but what is known already, yet is necessary to produce the death of Othello.

Had the scene opened in Cyprus, and the preceding incidents been occasionally related, there had been little wanting to a drama of the most exact and scrupulous regularity.

—Samuel Johnson, *The Plays of William Shakespeare* (London: J. & R. Tonson, 1765), Vol. 8, p. 472

✤

William Hazlitt on Characters and Dramatic Tension in *Othello*

[William Hazlitt (1778–1830) was one of the leading British essayists of the early nineteenth century. Among his many works are *Lectures on the English Poets* (1818), *Lectures on the English Comic Writers* (1819), *The Spirit of the Age* (1825), and a moving account of his love affair with a coquette, *Liber Amoris* (1823). In this extract from his important treatise, *Characters of Shakespear's Plays* (1817), Hazlitt remarks on the brilliance, both in characterization and in dramatic tension, of *Othello*.]

The picturesque contrasts of character in this play are almost as remarkable as the depth of the passion. The Moor Othello, the gentle Desdemona, the villain Iago, the good-natured Cassio, the fool Roderigo, present a range and variety of character as striking and palpable as that produced by the opposition of costume in a picture. Their distinguishing qualities stand out to the mind's eye, so that even when we are not thinking of their actions or sentiments, the idea of their persons is still as present to us as ever. These characters and the images they stamp upon the mind are the farthest asunder possible, the distance between them is immense: yet the compass of knowledge and invention which the poet has shown in embodying these extreme creations of his genius is only greater than the truth and felicity with which he has identified each character with itself, or blended their different qualities together in the same story. What a contrast the character of Othello forms to that of Iago! At the same time, the force of conception with which these two figures are opposed to each other is rendered still more intense by the complete consistency with which the traits of each character are brought out in a state of the highest finishing. The making one black and the other white, the one unprincipled, the other unfortunate in the extreme, would have answered the common purposes of effect, and satisfied the ambition of an ordinary painter of character. Shakespear has laboured the finer shades of difference in both with as much care and skill as if he had had to depend on the execution alone for the success of his design. On the other hand, Desdemona and Æmilia are not meant to be opposed with anything like strong contrast to each other. Both are, to outward appearance, characters of common life, not more distinguished than women usually are, by difference of rank and situation. The difference of their thoughts and sentiments is however laid open, their minds are separated from each other by signs as plain and as little to be mistaken as the complexions of their husbands.

The movement of the passion in Othello is exceedingly different from that of Macbeth. In Macbeth there is a violent struggle between opposite feelings, between ambition and the stings of conscience, almost from first to last: in Othello, the doubtful conflict between contrary passions, though dreadful, continues only for a short time, and the chief interest is excited by the alternate ascendancy of different passions, by the entire and unforeseen change from the fondest love and most unbounded confidence to the tortures of jealousy and the madness of hatred. The revenge of Othello, after it has once taken thorough possession of his mind, never quits it, but grows stronger and stronger at every moment of its delay. The nature of the Moor is noble, confiding, tender, and generous; but his blood is of the most inflammable kind; and being once roused by a sense of his wrongs, he is stopped by no considerations of remorse or pity till he has given a loose to all the dictates of his rage and his despair. It is in working his noble nature up to this extremity through rapid but gradual transitions, in raising passion to its height from the smallest beginnings and in spite of all obstacles, in painting the expiring conflict between love and hatred, tenderness and resentment, jealousy and remorse, in unfolding the strength and the weakness of our nature, in uniting sublimity of thought with the anguish of the keenest woe, in putting in motion the various impulses that agitate this our mortal being, and at last blending them in that noble tide of deep and sustained passion, impetuous but majestic, that 'flows on to the Propontic, and knows no ebb,' that Shakespear has shown the mastery of his genius and of his power over the human heart. The third act of Othello is his finest display, not of knowledge or passion separately, but of the two combined, of the knowledge of character with the expression of passion, of consummate art in the keeping up of appearances with the profound workings of nature, and the convulsive movements of uncontroulable agony, of the power of inflicting torture and of suffering it. Not only is the tumult of passion in Othello's mind heaved up from the very bottom of the soul, but [even] the slightest undulation of feeling is seen on the surface, as it arises from the impulses of imagination or the malicious suggestions of Iago. The progressive preparation for the catastrophe is wonderfully managed from the Moor's first gallant recital of the story of his love, of 'the spells and witchcraft he had used,' from his unlooked-for and romantic success, the fond satisfaction with which he dotes on his own happiness, the unreserved tenderness of Desdemona and her innocent importunities in favour of Cassio, irritating the suspicions instilled into her husband's mind by the perfidy of Iago, and rankling there to poison, till he loses all command of himself, and his rage can only be appeased by blood.

—William Hazlitt, *Characters of Shakespear's Plays* (1817), *The Complete Works of William Hazlitt*, ed. P. P. Howe (London: J. M. Dent & Sons, 1930), Vol. 4, pp. 200–202

Samuel Taylor Coleridge on Negroes and Moors

[Samuel Taylor Coleridge (1772–1834), aside from being one of the greatest British poets of the early nineteenth century, was also a penetrating critic. His most famous critical work is *Biographia Literaria* (1817). In 1819 he delivered a series of lectures on Shakespeare, which were published posthumously in his *Literary Remains* (1836–39). In this extract from that work, Coleridge unwittingly reveals his racial prejudice by maintaining that Shakespeare did not intend Othello to be a "negro" (a black African) but rather a Moor (an Arab from North Africa).]

Rod.: What a full fortune does the *thick-lips* owe,
If he can carry 't thus.

Roderigo turns off to Othello; and here comes one, if not the only, seeming justification of our blackamoor or negro Othello. Even if we supposed this an uninterrupted tradition of the theatre, and that Shakespeare himself, from want of scenes, and the experience that nothing could be made too marked for the senses of his audience, had practically sanctioned it,—would this prove aught concerning his own intention as a poet for all ages? Can we imagine him so utterly ignorant as to make a barbarous negro plead royal birth,—at a time, too, when negros were not known except as slaves?—As for Iago's language to Brabantio, it implies merely that Othello was a Moor, that is, black. Though I think the rivalry of Roderigo sufficient to account for his wilful confusion of Moor and Negro,—yet, even if compelled to give this up, I should think it only adapted for the acting of the day, and should complain of an enormity built on a single word, in direct contradiction to Iago's 'Barbary horse.' Besides, if we could in good earnest believe Shakespeare ignorant of the distinction, still why should we adopt one disagreeable possibility instead of a ten times greater and more pleasing probability? It is a common error to mistake the epithets applied by the *dramatis personæ* to each other, as truly descriptive of what the audience ought to see or know. No doubt Desdemona saw Othello's visage in his mind; yet, as we are constituted, and most surely as an English audience was disposed in the beginning of the seventeenth century, it would be something monstrous to conceive this beautiful Venetian girl falling in love with a veritable negro. It would argue a disproportionateness, a want of balance, in Desdemona, which Shakespeare does not appear to have in the least contemplated.

—Samuel Taylor Coleridge, "Notes on *Othello*" (1819), *Literary Remains*, ed. Henry Nelson Coleridge (London: William Pickering, 1836), Vol. 2, pp. 256–58

✤

A. C. Bradley on Iago's Motivations

[A. C. Bradley (1851–1935) was the leading British Shakespeare scholar of his time. He taught at the University of Liverpool, the University of Glasgow, and Oxford University and wrote *Oxford Lectures on Poetry* (1909) and *A Miscellany* (1929). In this extract, taken from his celebrated book, *Shakespearean Tragedy* (1904), Bradley studies the character of Iago, finding that the chief motivations for his actions are a longing for power and an artistic manipulation of human beings.]

Iago's longing to satisfy the sense of power is, I think, the strongest of the forces that drive him on. But there are two others to be noticed. One is the pleasure in an action very difficult and perilous and, therefore, intensely exciting. This action sets all his powers on the strain. He feels the delight of one who executes successfully a feat thoroughly congenial to his special aptitude, and only just within his compass; and, as he is fearless by nature, the fact that a single slip will cost him his life only increases his pleasure. His exhilaration breaks out in the ghastly words with which he greets the sunrise after the night of the drunken tumult which has led to Cassio's disgrace: 'By the mass, 'tis morning. Pleasure and action make the hours seem short.' Here, however, the joy in exciting action is quickened by other feelings. It appears more simply elsewhere in such a way as to suggest that nothing but such actions gave him happiness, and that his happiness was greater if the action was destructive as well as exciting. We find it, for instance, in his gleeful cry to Roderigo, who proposes to shout to Brabantio in order to wake him and tell him of his daughter's flight:

> Do, with like timorous accent and dire yell
> As when, by night and negligence, the fire
> Is spied in populous cities.

All through that scene; again, in the scene where Cassio is attacked and Roderigo murdered; everywhere where Iago is in physical action, we catch this sound of almost feverish enjoyment. His blood, usually so cold and slow, is racing through his veins.

But Iago, finally, is not simply a man of action; he is an artist. His action is a plot, the intricate plot of a drama, and in the conception and execution of it he experiences the tension and the joy of artistic creation. 'He is,' says Hazlitt, 'an amateur of tragedy in real life; and, instead of employing his invention on imaginary characters or long-forgotten incidents, he takes the bolder and more dangerous course of getting up his plot at home, casts the principal parts among his nearest friends and connections, and rehearses it in downright earnest, with steady nerves and unabated resolution.' Mr. Swinburne lays even greater stress on this aspect of Iago's character, and even declares that 'the very subtlest and strongest component of his complex nature' is 'the instinct of what Mr. Carlyle would call an inarticulate poet.' And those to whom this idea is unfamiliar, and who may suspect it at first sight of being fanciful, will find, if they examine the play in the light of Mr. Swinburne's exposition, that it rests on a true and deep perception, will stand scrutiny, and might easily be illustrated. They may observe, to take only one point, the curious analogy between the early stages of dramatic composition and those soliloquies in which Iago broods over his plot, drawing at first only an outline, puzzled how to fix more than the main idea, and gradually seeing it develop and clarify as he works upon it or lets it work. Here at any rate Shakespeare put a good deal of himself into Iago. But the tragedian in real life was not the equal of the tragic poet. His psychology, as we shall see, was at fault at a critical point, as Shakespeare's never was. And so his catastrophe came out wrong, and his piece was ruined.

Such, then, seem to be the chief ingredients of the force which, liberated by his resentment at Cassio's promotion, drives Iago from inactivity into action, and sustains him through it. And, to pass to a new point, this force completely possesses him; it is his fate. It is like the passion with which a tragic hero wholly identifies himself, and which bears him on to his doom. It is true that, once embarked on this course, Iago *could* not turn back, even if this passion did abate; and it is also true that he is compelled, by his success in convincing Othello, to advance to conclusions of which at the outset he did not dream. He is thus caught in his own web, and could not liberate himself if he would. But, in fact, he never shows a trace of wishing to do so, not a trace of hesitation, of looking back, or of fear, any more than of remorse; there is no ebb in the tide. As the crisis approaches there passes through his mind a fleeting doubt whether the deaths of Cassio and Roderigo are indispensable; but that uncertainty, which does not concern the main issue, is dismissed, and he goes forward with undiminished zest. Not even in his sleep—as in Richard's before his final battle—does any rebellion of outraged conscience or pity, or any foreboding of despair, force itself into clear consciousness. His fate—which is himself—has completely mastered him: so that, in the later scenes, where the improbability of the entire success of a design built on so many different falsehoods forces itself on the reader, Iago appears for moments not as a consummate schemer, but as a man absolutely infatuated and delivered over to certain destruction.

—A. C. Bradley, *Shakespearean Tragedy* (London: Macmillan, 1904), pp. 230–32

✤

Wyndham Lewis on Othello as Colossus

[Wyndham Lewis (1882–1957), whose career was advanced partly by his friend Ezra Pound, was the author of modernist novels (including *The Apes of God*, 1930) and a leading figure in the vorticist movement, which attacked the sentimentality of nineteenth-century art. Among his critical works are *Time and Western Man* (1927) and *The Lion and the Fox* (1927). In this extract from the latter work, Lewis argues that Othello is a typical Shakespearean colossus.]

Of all the colossi, Othello is the most characteristic, because he is the simplest, and he is seen in an unequal duel throughout with a perfect specimen of the appointed enemy of the giant—the representative of the race of men at war with the race of titans. The hero comes straight from a world where Machiavelli's black necessities—the obligation, for animal survival, for the lion to couple with the fox—are not known. He is absolutely defenceless: it is as though he were meeting one of his appointed enemies, disguised of course, as a friend, for the first time. He seems possessed of no instinct by which he might scent his antagonist, and so be put on his guard.

So, at the outset, I will present my version of Othello; and anything that I have subsequently to say must be read in the light of this interpretation. For in Othello there is nothing equivocal, I think; and the black figure of this child-man is one of the poles of Shakespeare's sensation.

Who that has read Othello's closing speech can question Shakespeare's intentions here at least? The overwhelming truth and beauty is the clearest expression of the favour of Shakespeare's heart and mind. Nothing that could ever be said would make us misunderstand what its author meant by it. Of all his ideal giants this unhappiest, blackest, most "perplexed" child was the one of Shakespeare's predilection.

The great spectacular "pugnacious" male ideal is represented perfectly by Othello; who was led out to the slaughter on the elizabethan stage just as the bull is thrust into the spanish bull-ring. Iago, the *taurobolus* of this sacrificial bull, the little David of this Goliath, or the little feat-gilded *espada,* is for Shakespeare nothing but Everyman, the Judas of the world, the representative of the crowds around the crucifix, or of the ferocious crowds at the *corrida,* or of the still more abject roman crowds at the mortuary games. Othello is of the race of Christs, or of the race of "bulls"; he is the hero with all the magnificent helplessness of the animal, or all the beauty and ultimate resignation of the god. From the moment he arrives on the scene of his execution, or when his execution is being prepared, he speaks with an unmatched grandeur and beauty. To the troop that is come to look for him, armed and snarling, he says: "Put up your bright swords or the dew will rust them!" And when at last he has been brought to bay he dies by that significant contrivance of remembering how he had defended the state when it was traduced, and in reviving this distant blow for his own demise. The great words roll on in your ears as the curtain falls:

> And say besides, that in Aleppo once. . . .

Iago is made to say:

> The Moor, howbeit that I endure him not,
> Is of a constant, loving, noble nature.

But we do not need this testimony to feel, in all our dealings with this simplest and grandest of his creations, that we are meant to be in the presence of an absolute purity of human guilelessness, a generosity as grand and unaffected, although quick and, "being wrought, Perplexed in the extreme," as deep as that of his divine inventor.

There is no utterance in the whole of Shakespeare's plays that reveals the nobleness of his genius and of its intentions in the same way as the speech with which Othello closes:

> Soft you; a word or two before you go.
> I have done the state some service, and they know it.
> No more of that. I pray you, in your letters,
> When you shall these unlucky deeds relate,
> Speak of me as I am; nothing extenuate,
> Nor set down aught in malice: then, must you speak
> Of one that loved, not wisely, but too well;
> Of one not easily jealous, but, being wrought,
> Perplex'd in the extreme; of one, whose hand,
> Like the base Indian, threw a pearl away,
> Richer than all his tribe; of one, whose subdued eyes,
> . . . .
> Drop tears as fast as the Arabian trees
> Their medicinal gum. Set you down this;
> And say, besides, that in Aleppo once,
> Where a malignant and a turban'd Turk
> Beat a Venetian, and traduced the state,
> I took by the throat the circumcisèd dog,
> And smote him—thus.

And it is the speech of a military hero, as simple-hearted as Hotspur. The tremendous and childlike pathos of this simple creature, broken by intrigue so easily and completely, is one of the most significant things for the comprehension of Shakespeare's true thought. For why should so much havoc ensue from the crude "management" of a very ordinary intriguer? It is no great devil that is pitted against him: and so much faultless affection is destroyed with such a mechanical facility. He is a toy in the hands of a person so much less real than himself; in every sense, human and divine, so immeasurably inferior.

> And say besides, that in Aleppo once.

This unhappy child, caught in the fatal machinery of "shakespearian tragedy," just as he might have been by an accident in the well-known world, remembers, with a measureless pathos, an event in the past to his credit, recalled as an afterthought, and thrown in at the last moment, a poor counter of "honour," to set against the violence to which he has been driven by the whisperings of things that have never existed.

And it is *we* who are intended to respond to these events, as the Venetian, Lodovico, does, when he apostrophizes Iago, describing him as:

> More fell than anguish, hunger or the sea!

The eloquence of that apostrophe is the measure of the greatness of the heart that we have seen attacked and overcome. We cannot take that as an eloquent outburst only: it was an expression of the author's conviction of the irreparable nature of the offence, because of the purity of the nature that had suffered. The green light of repugnance and judgment is thrown on to the small mechanical villain at the last.

—Wyndham Lewis, *The Lion and the Fox: The Role of the Hero in the Plays of Shakespeare* (New York: Harper & Brothers, 1927), pp. 190–93

✣

Kenneth Burke on Desdemona's Handkerchief

[Kenneth Burke (1897–1993) was a leading American literary critic and theorist as well as a poet. Among his critical works are *The Philosophy of Literary Forms* (1941), *A Grammar of Motives* (1945), and *Dramatism and Development* (1972). In this extract, Burke explores the symbolic use of Desdemona's handkerchief.]

"Sure, there's some wonder in this handkerchief," Desdemona had confided to Emilia; "I am most unhappy in the loss of it." And well she might be. For the handkerchief will sum up the entire complexity of motives. It will be public evidence of the conspiracy which Othello now wholly believes to exist (and which, according to our notions on the ironies of property, *does* exist). And by the same token, it will be the privacy of Desdemona made public. If she is enigmatic, emblematic, the gracious fetish not only of Othello, but of all who abide by these principles of spiritual ownership, then her capital as a woman is similarly representative, the emblem of her as emblem. Hence, this handkerchief that bridges realms, being the public surrogate of secrecy, it is an emblem's emblem—and in his belief that she had made a free gift of it to another, Othello feels a torrential sense of universal loss. Since it stands for Desdemona's privacy, and since this privacy in turn had stood magically for his entire sense of worldly and cosmological order, we can readily see why, for Othello, its loss becomes the ultimate obscenity. But there is a further point to be considered, thus:

Aristotle has said that accidents are best accepted in a tragedy when they are placed before the play's beginning, unless they can be made to seem fate-guided. Explicitly, there is no attempt here to show that the handkerchief is lost and found by supernatural guidance. The bluntness of the convenience is tempered by two devices of the plot: (1) Othello, by talking about it, calls the audience's clear attention to it when it falls; (2) since Emilia finds it and gives it to Iago, rather than Iago's finding it himself after having talked of wanting it, the addition of this intermediate step provides a certain tactful modulation between Desdemona's losing it and Iago's getting it. (Also, incidentally, this roundabout approach supplies complications that will later enable the plot to operate somewhat "of itself", when things must turn against the great impresario, Iago, Emilia having been given the information that leads to the exposing of him.)

But our main point is this: There is a kind of magic in the handkerchief, for the audience as well as for Othello—and this property serves as the *equivalent* of a fate-guided accident (the miraculous). It is this miraculous ingredient in the handkerchief that makes the audience willing to accept, so late in the play, the accident whereby Iago came into possession of it after giving notice that he wanted it. Or we'll state our position in modified form: Insofar as the accident is resented, the audience has not felt the equivalent for the fate-guided that we have in mind.

—Kenneth Burke, "*Othello:* An Essay to Illustrate a Method," *Hudson Review* 4, No. 2 (Summer 1951): 196–98

S. L. Bethell on Diabolism in *Othello*

[S. L. Bethell is a distinguished British scholar on Shakespeare and the author of *Shakespeare and the Popular Dramatic Tradition* (1944), *Essays on Literary Criticism and the English Tradition* (1948), and *The Cultural Revolution of the Seventeenth Century* (1957). In this extract, Bethell discusses the significance of diabolic images in *Othello*.]

How, then, are we to understand the great number of diabolic images in *Othello*? They are related closely to Iago, but in what way? I do not think that there is any Elizabethan convention by which the Machiavel or atheist is presented in such terms. I find only fourteen diabolic images in the whole of *The Atheist's Tragedy*: some are merely oaths and the rest have no great significance for character nor are they used to develop a theme. In *Othello* those employed by Iago himself are capable of naturalistic explanation up to a point. We might find credible the character of an evil man who, though an unbeliever, likes to dwell on that aspect of religion which fills others with dread and to model himself upon a Devil in whom he does not objectively believe. Alternatively, we could accept Iago as a 'practical atheist', one who lives by an atheistic code without making any deliberate intellectual rejection of religion. There are many such. If this were so, his enjoyment of the devilish might colour his language without implying either belief or disbelief. If naturalistic consistency of character is desired, I suppose that either of these readings might supply it. But Shakespeare leaves us small leisure for such speculation when we are watching *Othello*. What he does, however, is to assail our ears with diabolic imagery throughout, and by no means only in the speeches of Iago. A naturalistic solution is not quite impossible. Accepting either of the naturalistic explanations given above for Iago's use of this sort of imagery, we might argue that the other characters as they come into the circle of his influence take over his forms of expression. But would any Elizabethan, even Shakespeare, entertain such a notion—or even conceive such a character as either of the 'naturalistic' Iagos I have projected? Since we have established that Shakespeare's method was fundamentally conventional, there is no need to accept a fantastic naturalistic explanation if a plausible conventional explanation lies to hand.

I shall argue that the diabolic imagery is used to develop poetically an important underlying theme. Of the sixty-four diabolic images in *Othello* not one occurs in Cinthio's *novella.* We have found Shakespeare adding considerably to the number of religious images in the sources of *Macbeth* and sharpening those that were already there, so as to develop poetically a theological theme. Is it not likely that when he introduced a similar type of imagery into *Othello* it was with a similar purpose? There is a steady increase in the use of diabolic imagery from act to act, which looks like thematic development. The figures for each act are, respectively, ten, eleven, thirteen, fourteen, sixteen. I shall outline what I believe to be the general function of this imagery in *Othello* and then consider its operation in detail.

Othello can be interpreted on three levels, the personal, the social and the metaphysical. In *Lear* and *Macbeth* these three levels are so closely interrelated that it is impossible to make sense of the personal or story level without taking the others into consideration. In *Othello* the interrelationship is less complete: the story can be considered alone, with the result that the other elements often remain unnoticed. Unfortunately without them the story itself is liable to misinterpretation. On the personal level we have a straightforward domestic tragedy—Cinthio's *novella,* in fact, with modifications. On the social level we have a study of a contemporary problem, the clash between the 'new man' thrown up by certain aspects of Renaissance culture, the atheist-Machiavel with his principle of pure self-interest, and the chivalric type, representing the traditional values of social order and morality. That Iago is more intelligent than Othello reflects the usual ambivalence of Shakespeare's judgement. On the metaphysical level we see Othello and Iago as exemplifying and participating in the agelong warfare of Good and Evil.

These various planes of meaning coalesce into something like unity. It appears that to Shakespeare Cinthio's ensign suggested (*a*) the contemporary atheist-Machiavel, and (*b*) the Devil himself. It seems to follow that Shakespeare thought of the 'new man', with his contempt for traditional morality and religion, as a disintegrating force seeking to break down the social order that is a part of cosmic order—as, in fact, an instrument (no doubt unconscious) of the Devil in his constant effort to reduce cosmos to chaos. This would be a very natural attitude for a conservative Elizabethan, and to express this attitude is one main function—a general function—of the diabolic imagery in *Othello*: Iago is a "demi-devil" (V, ii, 301), worse than an ordinary devil, a bastard one, and his philosophy is a "divinity of hell".

—S. L. Bethell, "Shakespeare's Imagery: The Diabolic Images in *Othello*," *Shakespeare Survey* 5 (1952): 70–71

✤

W. H. Auden on Iago and Knowledge

[W. H. Auden (1907–1973) was one of the leading British poets of the twentieth century as well as an important critic. His best critical work is contained in *The Dyer's Hand and Other Essays* (1962), which contains several essays on Shakespeare. In this extract, Auden notes that we cannot condemn Iago utterly because he exhibits a quest for knowledge that we have come to regard as an absolute good.]

Iago's treatment of Othello conforms to Bacon's definition of scientific enquiry as putting Nature to the Question. If a member of the audience were to interrupt the play and ask him: "What are you doing?" could not Iago answer with a boyish giggle, "Nothing. I'm only trying to find out what Othello is really like"? And we must admit that his experiment is highly successful. By the end of the play he does know the scientific truth about the object to which he has reduced Othello. That is what makes his parting shot, "What you know, you know," so terrifying for, by then, Othello has become a thing, incapable of knowing anything.

And why shouldn't Iago do this? After all, he has certainly acquired knowledge. What makes it impossible for us to condemn him self-righteously is that, in our culture, we have all accepted the notion that the right to know is absolute and unlimited. The gossip column is one side of the medal; the cobalt bomb the other. We are quite prepared to admit that, while food and sex are good in themselves, an uncontrolled pursuit of either is not, but it is difficult for us to believe that intellectual curiosity is a desire like any other, and to realize that correct knowledge and truth are not identical. To apply a categorical imperative to knowing, so that, instead of asking, "What can I know?" we ask, "What, at this moment, am I meant to know?"—to entertain the possibility that the only knowledge which can be true for us is the knowledge we can live up to—that seems to all of us crazy and almost immoral. But, in that case, who are we to say to Iago—"No, you mustn't."

—W. H. Auden, "The Joker in the Pack" (1961), *The Dyer's Hand and Other Essays* (New York: Random House, 1962), pp. 271–72

K. W. Evans on Othello's Marriage

[K. W. Evans is a former lecturer in English literature at Ahmadu Bello University in Zaria, Nigeria. In this extract, Evans claims that Othello's marriage to Desdemona—and the racial hostility it engenders—is instrumental in bringing about his downfall.]

Although Othello's personal weaknesses ultimately cause his downfall, external factors beyond his previous experience also propel him towards tragic conflict, and it is necessary first to take close account of them before we can fully appreciate the reasons for Othello's collapse. A proper understanding of these pressures, and then of their effects, will show how important the question of race is in this play. *Othello* begins with news of what for most is a very strange marriage, and ends with its destruction. The characters react variously to the marriage, and these reactions set evil in motion. Before the marriage everyone liked both Desdemona and Othello, but after it few continue to admire Othello, and his sense of rejection increases until he attempts the life of one and kills the other of the two people who approve of him most. Criticisms of the married Othello are based mainly on racial considerations. Roderigo describes him as "the thicklips" (I.i.66), and shudders to think of Desdemona exposed "to the gross clasps of a lascivious Moor" (I.i.126). Emilia speaks of Desdemona's "most filthy bargain" (V.ii.158), and the illustrious general he was once pleased to entertain becomes "a thing" (I.ii.71) for Brabantio. True to his cast of mind, Iago calls Othello "a Barbary horse" (I.i.lll). The Duke's attitude towards the marriage is legalistic, and towards the bridegroom fair but not enthusiastic. All will praise the man, even Iago a little, but not the husband, and Othello becomes acutely aware that, despite his military rank, royal ancestry, and Christian faith, he is an alien in Venice.

Brabantio and Iago are particularly hostile towards the marriage, but although their views have much in common, the reasons for their behaviour are radically different. Brabantio's attitude is typical of certain contemporary feelings about the supposed inferiority of black Moors to Europeans. Othello's age is a small matter; it is the "unnaturalness" of the marriage that repels Brabantio. On his reckoning, Othello is simply a barbarian, and believing in a rigid natural hierarchy of men he will not judge Othello on his merits as a man of honour. Although he does not know Othello comes "from men of royal siege" (I.ii.22), it is certain that a negro aristocracy would not impress Brabantio. Whatever his rank in Venice and family in Africa, Othello remains a bond-slave in his eyes. Indeed, Brabantio almost speaks of the married pair as if they belonged to different species. Constantly he invokes his concept of nature. It is incredible that the daughter of a Venetian senator should love Othello. "Spells and medicines" (I.iii.61) have corrupted her; "for nature so preposterously to err . . . Sans witchcraft could not" (I.iii.62). How could she "in spite of nature . . . fall in love with what she fear'd to look on?" (I.iii.96); this would be "against all rules of nature" (I.iii.101). These rigid views rebound on Brabantio. Unwilling at first to think ill of his daughter, he speaks of deceit when she affirms her love, and later dies of sorrow. Given his opinion that the marriage is unnatural, it seems to follow that he reaches something like the same conclusion about her as Iago does by a different route.

No Venetian father would willingly allow his daughter to marry Othello, unless it were Rymer's "little drab or Small-coal Wench." This is why the lovers elope, and they will not be separated by crude insults. Their marriage is, however, more vulnerable to the subtle kind of enmity that inspires Iago. Although he shares the opinion of Moors held by most Venetians, his motives for action are not those of Brabantio; he opposes the match from the other end of the social scale, and not for reasons of virtuous indignation. In a very special sense, the marriage brings this normally insignificant man to life, and he comes to personify the more virulent aspects of Venetian prejudice against Moors. Although his hatred of Othello antedates the marriage, he acts upon his hatred now, because the very nature of the marriage excites the feelings of sexual and social envy that govern his character. The compulsive nature of these feelings is clear from the brief airing Iago gives to his personal grievances, and then, for the most part, forgets. So, his suspicions about Emilia's relations with Cassio and Othello derive from the same sense of sexual inadequacy as his frustrated desire for Desdemona, prompted solely by her marriage to a Moor of all people. Sensitivity about social status is also a potent factor in Iago's character. A probable belief that his betters think him too dull to be anything but honest, his delighted references to others' stupidity coupled with pride in his own cleverness, his eager fastening onto this chance to pull down his superiors, and his need of a Roderigo as confidant, point to a deep feeling of social inferiority, which the matter of the lieutenancy merely confirms. In this Venice, one of Iago's kind will inevitably be outraged by an Othello daring to aspire to such heights; equally he is sure to conclude that Desdemona is not as refined as she looks. Iago would, of course, envy the happiness of any pair of lovers, but it takes this extraordinary union between Moorish sensuality and feigned Venetian gentility, which is all the marriage means to Iago, to stimulate an awareness of his own amorous and worldly shortcomings to a maximum. Emilia's mistress, with all her airs and graces, marrying a man like that! Brabantio may declare that Desdemona is too good for Othello, but Iago will say that she is bad enough for any man, because this allows him to despise both the lovers. And Iago is sure that Othello is a credulous and violently jealous fool like all Africans, who can easily be roused to pitiless fury by the unworthiness imputed to him, so that Iago may hope at one blow to placate both the kinds of inferiority that plague him. This marriage, in fact, is a challenge to Iago's very meaning, and as racial prejudice links up with those deeper feelings to which it points in his case, Iago acquires a force that takes him well beyond the sum of his declared motives.

—K. W. Evans, "The Racial Factor in *Othello*," *Shakespeare Studies* 5 (1969): 126–28

✤

Stanley Edgar Hyman on Iago as Slighted Homosexual

[Stanley Edgar Hyman (1919–1970), the husband of fiction writer Shirley Jackson, was a noted literary critic and reviewer. Among his works are *The Armed Vision: A Study in the Methods of Modern Literary Criticism* (1948), *Nathanael West* (1962), and *Flannery O'Connor* (1966). In this extract from his study of Iago, Hyman maintains that Iago's homosexual feelings for Othello help motivate his destruction of the Moor.]

This approach is psychoanalytic criticism, and its Iago is motivated by strong latent homosexuality (or acts as does a person so motivated). This is not only abundantly clear in the play, but it is clearly of Shakespeare's deliberate contrivance, since there is no trace of any such thing in the story he got from his source, Giovanbattista Giraldi Cinthio's *Hecatommithi,* and all the evidences of it in the play are Shakespeare's alterations and additions. In Cinthio's tale, the Ensign falls passionately in love with Disdemona, and he really does believe that she loves the Cassio character; he is, in short, motivated by normal heterosexual jealousy. Iago neither loves Desdemona nor believes for a moment that she loves Cassio, despite several statements he makes to the contrary. It is he who unconsciously loves both Othello and Cassio; that love is repressed and, by the defense mechanism called "reaction formation," turned into hate.

In the first scene of the first act, Iago expresses his hostility to Cassio, as knowing nothing more of battles "then a Spinster" and as "almost damn'd in a faire Wife," curious terms for a handsome and virile bachelor; and he twice strongly denies any affection for Othello in speeches already quoted, "not I for love" in the heart-on-the-sleeve speech, and again in the speech punning on "sign." Another ingredient of Iago's strong latent homosexuality is his contempt for women and his disgust with heterosexual love and marriage, both themes pervading the play. The line about Cassio, "almost damn'd in a faire Wife," is quite interesting in this connection. Whether it means, as the Cowden-Clarkes understood it, "A fellow who would almost go to perdition for a handsome woman," or, as J. J. B. Workard explained it, " 'fellow' of so soft a character that a similar disposition would be 'almost damned in a fair wife,' " the views of women are equally scornful, and if it means what Steevens thought (and Malone concurred in), "he is not yet *completely damned,* because he is not *absolutely married,*" the view of marriage is no more lovely. The scene also contains a number of clear evidences of Iago's disgust with heterosexuality itself, which he tends to put in bestial imagery, as he does throughout the play (expressing what Heilman calls Iago's "barnyard view of life"). Iago cries up to Brabantio, "an old blacke Ram / Is tupping your white Ewe," then continues

> . . . you'le have your Daughter cover'd with a Barbary horse, you'le have your Nephewes neigh to you, you'le have Coursers for Cozens: and Gennets for Germaines.

His final remark along these lines is the most gross, "your Daughter and the Moore, are making the Beast with two backs."

In the second scene, telling Cassio the news about Othello, Iago changes his metaphor, informing him "he to night hath boarded a Land Carract," which Staunton explains as a large ship like a Spanish galleon, adding, "the compound in the text appears to have been a dissolute expression."

In the third scene, alone with Rodorigo, Iago combines the two sorts of imagery. He proclaims: "Ere I would say, I would drowne my selfe for the love of a Ginney Hen, I would change my Humanity with a Baboone," and Steevens explains "guinea hen" as "Anciently the cant term for a prostitute." Iago continues with an assurance to Rodorigo of the sort that he uses regularly to dupe him, but here in a psychoanalytic perspective we have to see a powerful unconscious wish underlying the duping. "It cannot be long that Desdemona should continue her love to the Moore," he says, "nor he his to her. . . . These Moores are changeable in their wils." Iago goes on to state his own emotional investment in the matter (more than he realizes). He says, "I have told thee often, and I re-tell thee againe, and againe, I hate the Moore. . . . If thou canst Cuckold him, thou dost thy selfe a pleasure, me a sport." After Rodorigo has been sent off, Iago has his soliloquy to conclude the act, and tells the audience:

> I hate the Moore,
> And it is thought abroad, that 'twixt my sheets
> He ha's done my Office.

(Heilman comments excellently on the inadequacy of that "and" in place of the expected "since.") This charge, which is patently untrue, is flatly contradicted by other things that Iago says of Othello, and after one more repetition in Act II, scene 1, is entirely forgotten. Such unconvincing explanations, dismissed by other approaches as either Coleridge's "motive-hunting" or as the same sort of lying to the audience as Iago's lying to Rodorigo, have great significance in a psychoanalytic perspective. They reflect the unconscious wish that Othello go to bed with him, disguised by projection as the possibility that Othello has gone to bed with Æmilia, and further defended against by being made rumor rather than his own idea. More deeply, they show the characteristic "castration anxiety" or "negative Oedipus complex," which is one of the possible reactions to the Oedipal ambivalence toward the father, in which the active or strongly latent homosexual identifies with his mother or a mother-surrogate and in fantasy enjoys his father sexually. Othello takes Iago's place with his wife as the more virile and dominant figure; in another aspect, it is the common latent homosexual fantasy, obsessive in the work of Joyce, of two men symbolically uniting sexually by sharing the body of the same woman.

—Stanley Edgar Hyman, *Iago: Some Approaches to the Illusion of His Motivation* (New York: Atheneum, 1970), pp. 101–5

✣

Leslie A. Fiedler on Cassio

[Leslie A. Fiedler (b. 1917), the Samuel L. Clemens Professor of Literature at the State University of New York at Buffalo, is a leading American literary critic and advocate of the literary and cultural significance of popular literature. Among his many books are *Waiting for the End* (1964), *The Return of the Vanishing American* (1968), *Collected Essays* (1971), and *What Was Literature? Class Culture and Mass Society* (1982). In this extract from *The Stranger in Shakespeare* (1972), Fiedler examines the character of Cassio, who degenerates into a maudlin drunkard in the course of the play.]

Cassio, on the other hand, is not funny at all, becoming sloppily religious when under the influence and solemnly reciting antialcoholic platitudes when sobering up. "Every inordinate cup is unblest, and the ingredient is a devil." To this, Iago responds, as is his wont, with counter-commonplaces. "Come, come, good wine is a good familiar creature, if it be well used. Exclaim no more against it. . . . You or any man living may be drunk at some time, man." Yet in this play, only Cassio is shown really drunk; and, indeed, his drunkenness marks the beginning of the catastrophe. Being cashiered as a result, he turns to Iago, who suggests he work on Othello through Desdemona, since, he assures him, "Our General's wife is now the General." But this feeds Othello's paranoid fantasies, thus releasing the second "devil" of Cyprus: "the green-eyed monster which doth mock / The meat it feeds on," and turning one "not easily jealous" into a near maniac, who, rising from an epileptic "ecstasy," shouts at his suspected wife, "I am glad to see you mad." What he means, apparently, but cannot otherwise confess, is: I am mad to see you glad; and as if to prove it, he slaps her face in the presence of a visiting Venetian dignitary, her father's kinsman.

The downward transformation of Cassio on Cyprus is not so spectacular, perhaps, but quite as drastic; for he becomes an affected maker of exaggerated compliments, a snatcher of kisses a shade more ardent than courtesy allows, a mocker at fond and foolish women, and of course, a bad drunk, first boastful, then violent, and at last maudlin. What he was before we can only surmise from the fact that Othello had preferred him for a lieutenancy to begin with, and that, at the play's end, the Senators of Venice have appointed him governor in Othello's place. We see almost nothing of him in Act I, in which he serves only as a messenger between the Moor and the Senate; and he seems (or acts?) totally ignorant of the connection between Othello and Desdemona, asking "To who?" when Iago tells him the Moor is married. Later, however, we learn from Desdemona that Cassio had actually come "a-wooing" with his general, even defending him against her playful attacks. Shakespeare seems, as a matter of fact, more than a little uncertain about just who Michael Cassio is, speaking of him on various occasions as if he were a Florentine, a Venetian, and a Veronese; and seeming to change his mind about whether or not he is, like his prototype in Cinthio, married.

The first reference to him is by Iago, who speaks of "Michael Cassio, a Florentine, / a fellow almost damned in a fair wife"; but clearly he is intended to be a bachelor when he reappears on Cyprus. The phrase is, however, fascinating in its own right, since it represents the initial use of the key word "fair" in a play, for which it would, indeed, provide an apt epigraph, if we took it to refer to Othello rather than Cassio. Certainly, it has long troubled the commentators, though perhaps it can be read—wrenching the syntax only a little—as meaning almost damned by a weakness for other men's fair wives. And in that case, Iago's later description of Cassio as one ". . . framed to make women false" could serve as a gloss upon it.

He should, in any event, be played with a touch of irony, for he is a shade too familiar with Emilia, a shade too courtly with Desdemona, and much too cold-blooded in his trifling with Bianca to seem wholly sympathetic, however unfairly he is treated by Othello. And when, totally under the influence, he insists to Iago that in heaven itself he will outrank him still ("Aye, but, by your leave. . . . the Lieutenant is to be saved before the Ancient"), we are tempted momentarily to side with the snubbed villain. Indeed, it seems possible that though Cassio's line of descent runs back through Bassanio all the way to the young man of the *Sonnets,* this time Shakespeare himself is a little wary of his professional charm. Certainly he bestows on him no happy ending except a better job, but this his sources and the tragic form had predetermined, leaving no suitable woman alive at the action's end.

—Leslie A. Fiedler, *The Stranger in Shakespeare* (New York: Stein & Day, 1972), pp. 187–89

✤

RUTH NEVO ON IAGO'S HOSTILITY TO OTHELLO

[Ruth Nevo (b. 1924), formerly a professor of English at the University of Jerusalem, is the author of *Comic Transformations in Shakespeare* (1980) and *Shakespeare's Other Language* (1987). In this extract from *Tragic Form in Shakespeare* (1972), Nevo ponders the causes of Iago's hostility to Othello, concluding that chief among these is his racial prejudice.]

If Iago's open and palpable villainy makes the answer to the question "Whence evil?" easy to answer, the total predicament presented in Act I is anything but simple. It possesses the peculiar complexity that is characteristic of the mature tragedies: the knotting of past with future, of the fatalities that have already shaped the protagonist's circumstances and character with those on the brink of which he stands. It is, in ⟨Erich⟩ Auerbach's phrase, "fraught with background." What makes Othello's situation challenging and testing is the fact, salient, specific, and plain for all to see, that Othello is a Moor. This circumstance complicates Othello's role both as soldier and as lover, and is brought into prominence in many ways. The very title of the play points to the focal prominence of Othello's ethnic origin, and it is manifest in the theatrical spectacle itself. He is singled out, this extravagant and wheeling stranger, this erring barbarian, redoubtable soldier-servant of the Venetian state, as physically distinguished from those about him, as alien and unique. This Moor has risen to command the respect of the subtlest and most sophisticated of cities in its most vulnerable point: defense. This erstwhile pagan has transcended his wild Berber ancestry to become the shield of the Venetian city against the menace of the Turkish infidel.

The entire presentation of Othello in the first act is geared to this perception of him, and it is in this light that both Iago's contemptuous references to black rams and Barbary horses and Othello's exotic evocation of antres vast and deserts idle, his free unhoused condition and his descent from men of royal siege, become fully operative in the dramatic scheme. Both sets of associations existed in the Elizabethan imagination: blackamoors, bondslaves, and pagans—barbarians both menacing and repulsive; and the romantic or chivalric wild Berber chiefs. The strategy of the opening raises the highest expectations concerning his entrance, his performance. Iago's coarse denigration; the facts and the mysteries of the elopement; Brabantio's distress; the foolish Roderigo, who, as rival suitor to Desdemona, suggests a contrast of some kind; all these intensify expectation for that first sight of Othello himself. Such heightened expectation is in any case inherent in the universal human spectrum of possible responses (from xenophobia to love of the exotic) to the outsider; and this expectation is the source of the breathtaking effectiveness of "Keep up your bright swords, for the dew will rust 'em" when the single commanding figure subdues the excited Venetian burghers with one ineradicable gesture of composed authority. The exhibition of Othello's impressive authority, control, and dignity, his unflinching sense of his own worth, strikes upon the sensibility of the audience in this context of expectation, establishing the image of a figure who is the composed embodiment of a unique triumph.

—Ruth Nevo, *Tragic Form in Shakespeare* (Princeton: Princeton University Press, 1972), pp. 183–85

SUSAN SNYDER ON DESDEMONA'S LOVE FOR OTHELLO

[Susan Snyder (b. 1934) is a professor of English and head of the department at Swarthmore College. She has produced an edition of *All's Well That Ends Well* (1993) and has written *The Comic Matrix of Shakespeare's Tragedies* (1979), from which the following extract is taken. Here, Snyder shows that Desdemona defies conventional views of "nature" in her love for Othello.]

If reason's opposition to love is traditional, nature in *Othello* appears to have changed sides. Love's ally is now love's enemy, partly because the angle of vision has changed: nature as instinctual rightness gives way to nature as abstract concept, susceptible like all concepts to distortion and misapplication. Brabantio, Iago, and finally Othello himself see the love between Othello and Desdemona as *un*natural—"nature erring from itself" (III.iii.231). But there is more to it than this. In key scenes of *Othello* a tension develops between two senses of *nature,* the general and the particular.

It is to general nature, the common experience and prejudice by which like calls only to like, that Brabantio appeals in the Venetian council scene. An attraction between the young white

Venetian girl and the aging black foreigner, since it goes against this observed law of nature, could only have been "wrought" by unnatural means.

> She is abus'd, stol'n from me, and corrupted,
> By spells and medicines bought of mountebanks;
> For nature so preposterously to err,
> Being not deficient, blind, or lame of sense,
> Sans witchcraft could not. (I.iii.60–64)

The other sense of *nature* is particular and personal. What Iago means in his soliloquy at the end of this scene when he says the Moor "is of a free and open nature" is individual essence: the inscape of Othello. Brabantio tries to bring in this nature to support the other in his appeal against the marriage. He says that Desdemona is essentially timid, thus by nature (her own) cannot love the fearsome Moor.

> A maiden never bold,
> Of spirit so still and quiet that her motion
> Blush'd at herself; and she—in spite of nature,
> Of years, of country, credit, every thing—
> To fall in love with what she fear'd to look on!
> It is a judgment maim'd and most imperfect
> That will confess perfection so could err
> Against all rules of nature. (I.iii.94–101)

But this personal nature is the very ground of Desdemona's love. In her answer to her father and the Venetian Senate she tells how, penetrating through the blackness and strangeness, she saw Othello's true visage in his mind and subdued her heart to that essence, his "very quality."

For Desdemona, then, nature as individual essence is not the enemy of love. But Iago has the last word in this scene, and his conclusion is ominous: Othello's very generosity and openness will make him take the appearance of honesty for the fact. That is, Othello will act instinctively according to the laws of his own nature rather than according to reasoned evaluation (which would perceive that most liars pretend to be telling the truth). This internal law of nature, then, implies the same vulnerability that we have seen in the instinctive, nonrational quality of Othello's and Desdemona's love.

Brabantio's general nature is implicitly reductive in that it derives rules for individuals from the behavior of the herd. Iago's is explicitly reductive. For him "the herd" is no metaphor, and the view he expounds to Roderigo has no place for human values or ethical norms. Natural law for Iago, as for Edmund in *King Lear*, is Hobbesian—a matter of animal appetites promoted by cleverness, with the strongest and the shrewdest winning out. Desdemona, he assures Roderigo, will tire of Othello because the appetite requires fresh stimuli:

> Her eye must be fed; and what delight shall she have to look on the devil? When the blood is made dull with the act of sport, there should be—again to inflame it, and to give satiety a fresh appetite—loveliness in favour, sympathy in years, manners, and beauties—all which the Moor is defective in. Now for want of these requir'd conveniences, her delicate tenderness will find itself abus'd, begin to heave the gorge, disrelish and abhor the Moor; very nature will instruct her in it, and compel her to some second choice. (II.i.221–233)

Compel her—here is yet another "law," generalized from the ways of animal nature. The context is wholly physical, as the persistent images of eating and disgorging keep reminding us. Iago has begun the discussion by prodding on the hesitant lover Roderigo with a bit of folk wisdom: "They say base men being in love have then a nobility in their natures more than is native to them" (212–214). But he does not pretend to believe it himself. Love is rather "a lust of the blood and a permission of the will"; Roderigo, in love or not, is a snipe; our natures are "blood and baseness." In Iago's determined animalism there is another unexpected reminder of comedy, this time of the antiromantic servant or rustic whose imagination is bounded by the physical. It is perhaps because this view can be destructive when actually *acted out* against idealized love that the clowns of comedy are kept largely apart from the plot, as onlookers. Iago is a clown without good humor and (what underlies that lack) without self-sufficiency, who must therefore prove his theories on other people. Interestingly, this transfer of the debunking low-life perspective to the service of active malevolence seems to have left no function for the play's official clown. His feeble essays at bawdry and wordplay have nothing conceptual to adhere to, and after a second brief appearance in Act II he departs unmourned.

—Susan Snyder, *The Comic Matrix of Shakespeare's Tragedies:* Romeo and Juliet, Hamlet, Othello, *and* King Lear (Princeton: Princeton University Press, 1979), pp. 77–80

✤

JOHN BAYLEY ON LOVE AND SEX IN *OTHELLO*

[John Bayley (b. 1925) is a distinguished British critic of English and Russian literature. Among his many works are *The Romantic Survival* (1957), *The Characters of Love* (1960), and *Housman's Poems* (1992). In this extract from *Shakespeare and Tragedy* (1981), Bayley asserts that much of the dramatic conflict in *Othello* rests upon the division between love and sex.]

Shakespeare generally does not in the least distinguish between love and sex: *Romeo and Juliet* shows that. Both in comedy and tragedy the two go naturally and properly together, for men and women alike. Claudius and Gertrude, as much as Portia and Bassanio, have their sexual tenderness as well as love for each other taken for granted; even when, as in the latter case, marriage is a combination of fairy story and business arrangement. But in reconstructing and re-imagining the Othello story for his play Shakespeare had to divorce love from sex as a logical result of separating the romantic nobility of Othello from the underworld intrigue of Iago. The only characters for whom love and sex are taken for granted as parts of the same whole are the three women, Bianca, Emilia, and Desdemona herself.

The consequences of this are bound to be striking, and indeed they are at the root of our divided apprehension of the Othello world and the Iago world. The explicit presence of sex as a kind of basic sport, intrigue and power struggle, whereas love is a lofty affair of adventure and romance, gives the play an atmosphere as much Victorian as Elizabethan, and this goes with its popularity in the nineteenth century after Kean's revival. Historically, men do tend to separate love and sex and to regard both as their due, but in different contexts. Where Shakespeare himself is concerned, a sense of the division, and the need to compensate for it with some bridging material, are shown by his emphasis on the pungent common sense of Emilia, and the no less cheerful and sensible temper of Desdemona, which she displays in conversation with the two officers before Othello's arrival in Cyprus.

Impossible of course to say how the division declared itself to the artist: it might seem his imaginative reaction to the idea of two men who are locked in this dramatic relationship. In Cinthio's tale the relation is in every way more ordinary, and has a kind of low-key plausibility. The commander waits in anxious suspense for days for the proofs of his wife's infidelity which his subordinate has promised to obtain. When convinced, he enters with him into an ingenious conspiracy to make the murder look like an accident, caused by a fall of plaster from the ceiling. Between the pair there is none of the gap between the lover and the connoisseur of sex, no sharp division in outlook. Both indeed in their way have had ample opportunity to feel love for the murdered wife, the ensign because of his infatuation with her, and the general because he has been for a long time a tender and happy husband. 'Their affection was . . . mutual.' 'No word passed between them that was not affectionate and kind.' This makes the crime more dreadful but also in its way more probable. The confusion and duplicity, hatred and sorrow, take place not only in the world of a newspaper story but are narrated in order to point a moral, or rather several, about the evils of credulity and gossip, and of marrying outside one's race and community.

Shakespeare's drastic simplification of the bond between commander and subordinate has the effect of squeezing out the onlooker, who can take part, as it were, neither in terms of love as Othello sees it or in terms of sex as Iago does. The pair drag into their area of high tension the habitual concordances of sex and love, and split them violently asunder. Othello's response to Iago's first tentative hints have led the critics, who see him as a study in the vulnerability of egotism, to claim that he meets Iago half-way and makes his work easy and its plausibility absolute. There is truth in this in so far as Iago's suggestions are all about sex, for the mention of sex in connection with the woman he loves is an explosive subject to Othello. The inability to conceive of one in terms of another, where she is concerned, and himself in terms of both, is at the root of the disaster. None the less love and sex, and the barrier between them, not only squeeze out the onlooker from the play: they also squeeze out tragedy. But the variety of ways in which that happens is always an asset to the Shakespearean work of art.

—John Bayley, *Shakespeare and Tragedy* (London: Routledge & Kegan Paul, 1981), pp. 209–10

Carol Thomas Neely on the Contrast Between Men and Women in *Othello*

[Carol Thomas Neely (b. 1939), a professor of English at the University of Illinois, has coedited *The Woman's Part: Feminist Criticism of Shakespeare* (1980) and written *Broken Nuptials in Shakespeare's Plays* (1985), from which the following extract is taken. Here, Neely finds stark contrasts between the men in *Othello* (who are murderous and lustful) and the women (who are realistic and balanced).]

The men in *Othello* extend and darken the anxieties of the comedy heroes. They are, in Emilia's words, "murderous coxcombs" (V.ii.234). Three out of the five attempt murder; five out of the five are foolish and vain. Roderigo, most obviously a coxcomb, shows in exaggerated fashion the dangerous combination of romanticism and misogyny and the dissociation of love and sex that all the men share. He is a parody of the conventional Petrarchan lover: love is a "torment," death a "physician" (I.iii.308–09), Desdemona "full of most blest condition" (II.i.247), and consummation of their relationship securely impossible. Yet he easily accepts Desdemona's supposed adultery and the necessity of Cassio's murder; his casual cynicism comes to outdo Iago's: " 'Tis but a man gone" (V.i.10). The other men have similarly divided and possessive views of women. Brabantio shifts abruptly from protective affection for the chaste Desdemona—"of spirit / So still and quiet, that her motion/Blush'd at her self" (I.iii.94–96)—to physical revulsion from the assertive sexuality revealed by her elopement—"I had rather to adopt a child than get it" (I.iii.191). Cassio's divided view is more conventionally accommodated. He idealizes the "divine Desdemona," flirting courteously and cautiously with her and rejecting Iago's insinuations about her sexuality; this side of women is left to Bianca, who is a "monkey" and a "fitchew" and is used and degraded for it. Othello's conflict regarding women is more profound, and the other men's solutions are not open to him. Because of his marriage and his integrity, he cannot, like Roderigo, assert Desdemona's chastity and corruptibility simultaneously; like Cassio, direct his divided emotions toward different objects; or, like Brabantio, disown the problem. ⟨. . .⟩

The women in *Othello* are not murderous, nor are they foolishly idealistic or anxiously cynical, as the men are. From the start they, like the comedy heroines, combine realism with romance, mockery with affection. Bianca comically reflects the qualities of the women as Roderigo does those of the men. The play associates her with the other two women by means of the overheard conversation about her which Othello takes to be about Desdemona and by means of her irate and essentially just response to Emilia's attack: "I am no strumpet, but of life as honest / As you, that thus abuse me" (V.i.120–21). At this point, Iago tries to fabricate evidence against her, just as Othello, in the scene immediately following, fabricates a case against Desdemona. Bianca's active, open-eyed enduring affection is similar to that of the other women. She neither romanticizes love nor degrades sex. She sees Cassio's callousness but accepts it wryly—" 'Tis very good, I must be circumstanc'd" (III.iv.199). She mocks him to his face but not behind his back, as he does her. Her active pursuit of Cassio is in contrast to his indifference, to Roderigo's passivity, and to Othello's naiveté. Even when jealous, she continues to feel affection for Cassio, accusing him openly and demanding that he come to dinner on her terms. The play's humanization of her, much like, for example, that of the bourgeois characters at the end of *Love's Labor's Lost,* underlines the folly of the male characters (and critics) who see her as merely a whore.

Emilia articulates the balanced view that Bianca embodies—"and though we have some grace, / Yet have we some revenge" (IV.iii.92–93). She, like other Shakespearean shrews, especially Beatrice and Paulina, combines sharp-tongued honesty with warm affection. Her views are midway between Desdemona's and Bianca's and between those of the women and those of the men. She rejects the identification with Bianca yet sympathizes with female promiscuity. She corrects Desdemona's occasional naiveté but defends her chastity. Although she comprehends male jealousy and espouses sexual equality, she seems remarkably free from jealousy herself. She wittily sees cuckoldry and marital affection as compatible: "Who would not make her husband a cuckold, to make him a monarch?" (IV.iii.74–75). She understands, but tolerates, male fancy; the dangers of such tolerance become evident in this play as they never do in the comedies.

—Carol Thomas Neely, *Broken Nuptials in Shakespeare's Plays* (New Haven: Yale University Press, 1985), pp. 111–12, 114–15

✣

ANTHONY HECHT ON THE CHRISTIANIZED MOOR

[Anthony Hecht (b. 1923) is a noted American poet, critic, and lecturer. His critical work has been gathered in *Obbligati* (1986), which contains a lecture on *Othello* from which the following extract is taken. Here, Hecht investigates the odd predicament of being a Moor in Venice and reflects on the significance of Othello's Christianity.]

It seems to me evident that an Elizabethan audience would not have been willing to grant Othello the unlimited admiration he receives from Cassio, Desdemona, the Duke, and his senate at the beginning of the play. He would have been recognized from the start as an anomaly, not only "an extravagant and wheeling stranger/Of here and everywhere," who has no real home, and therefore no civic allegiance, but, far more suspiciously, one who, had things only been slightly different (and perhaps more normal) would have been fighting on the enemy side, with the Turks and against the Venetians. Not only are we invited to share this edgy feeling, we are led to believe that Othello himself is not quite at ease in any society except that of military action, and his uneasiness is expressed, now and again, in a baroque and unnecessarily contorted syntax and diction. His manner of speech is remarked on within the first fifteen lines of the play by Iago, who speaks contemptuously of his "bombast circumstances/Horribly stuff'd with epithets of war." But it is not only to military matters that this eccentricity applies. Othello's first speech in the play (aside from a brief half-line) is an example of the sort of knotted constructions that stand out as ungainly and unnatural. In response to Iago's warning that Brabantio is rousing sentiments against Othello's marriage, Othello declares,

> Let him do his spite.
> My services, which I have done the signiory,
> Shall out-tongue his complaints; 'tis yet to know—
> Which, when I know that boasting is an honour,
> I shall promulgate—I fetch my life and being
> From men of royal siege, and my demerits
> May speak unbonneted to as proud a fortune
> As this that I have reach'd; for know, Iago,
> But that I love the gentle Desdemona,
> I would not my unhoused free condition
> Put into circumscription and confine
> For the sea's worth.

I submit that this is far from straightforward speech, and in it is couched no mere self-respect, nor even boasting under the guise of refusing to boast, but what I think was meant to be immediately recognized as a ludicrous and nervous vanity. We get no more about Othello's genealogy, nor any glimpse of his family life, since by his own admission he was given over to the profession of war from the age of seven. But to claim that the cream of Moorish society was the equal of the best of Venetian nobility would probably have provoked the sort of smile based on racial and national snobbery that has a central place in this play. "Unbonneted" occurs nowhere else in the entire Shakespeare corpus, and would normally mean taking the bonnet *off* as a sign of obeisance before a superior. In the present context, as has been noted, it must mean *without* taking the bonnet off, since Othello is insisting that he need defer to no one. Either he is using an exoticism with which we are unfamiliar, or he is misusing the language. There is, in any case, a manifest self-consciousness about his speech, with its intricate pattern of " 'tis yet to know, . . . which, when I know . . . for know, Iago," that marks it off from the speech of all others in the play—except Iago's when, out of malicious pleasure and spite, he parodies Othello to his face in speeches Othello is too preoccupied to recognize as parody, but which we are free to notice. I shall take note of these in due course. We have the unassailable fact of Othello's Moorishness, a fact conventionally assimilated to negroid features, and undisguisedly identified with black skin ("an old black ram/Is tupping your white ewe") and about which, since it cannot be concealed, Othello appears to be defensively proud.

But Othello is not simply a Moor; he is a Christian, and the play abounds with imagery of Christian salvation and damnation, and in the almost continuous confrontation of heaven and hell. When Othello offers to tell the story of his courtship, and reveal what magic charms he has used to win Desdemona (a taunt he is delighted to prove baseless and show that he is more sophisticated than to dabble in such primitive rites) he sends Iago to bring Desdemona to testify for herself, and says,

> And till she come, as truly as to heaven
> I do confess the vices of my blood,
> So justly to your grave ears I'll present
> How I did thrive in this fair lady's love,
> And she in mine.

It had best be said immediately that the quarto substitutes "faithful" for "truly," and omits the entire line, "I do confess the vices of my blood." But that line is by no means the only index of Othello's Christian orientation. Addressing the Duke and senators he swears, "Vouch with me, heaven," and says to them, "heaven defend your good souls." Agreeing to

Desdemona's prayer that their marital happiness may continue and grow, he declares, "Amen to that, sweet powers!" More explicitly still, when called from his marriage bed by the brawl of Cassio and Roderigo, he calls everyone to order in the following terms:

> Why, how now, ho! From whence ariseth this?
> Are we turned Turks, and to ourselves do that
> Which heaven hath forbid the Ottomites?
> For Christian shame put by this barbarous brawl!

There would, I venture to suppose, be something slightly galling to an Elizabethan audience in having a Moor lecture his gentile associates and subordinates on Christian behavior. If "turn Turk" means "turn renegade," one wonders what this might have meant, coming from the mouth of a Moor, since the Moor himself must have turned renegade to become a Christian. He is, in all probability, a Morisco, or New Christian, a breed regarded without much trust by the Christian community at that time.

—Anthony Hecht, *"Othello," Obbligati: Essays in Criticism* (New York: Atheneum, 1986), pp. 60–63

✤

EDWARD BERRY ON OTHELLO AND RACISM

[Edward Berry (b. 1940) is a professor of English and dean of humanities at the University of Victoria in British Columbia. He has written *Patterns of Decay: Shakespeare's Early Histories* (1975) and *Shakespeare's Comic Rites* (1984). In this extract, Berry studies the effects on Othello of the clear racial prejudice exhibited by other characters.]

To understand Othello's predicament, one must appreciate not only his "Africanness" but his position as a black man in Venetian society; he is the Moor of Venice. The fact of Othello's alienation is the play's most striking visual effect. One can imagine something of the original impact upon Shakespeare's audience by viewing the Longleat drawing of a scene from *Titus Andronicus*, reproduced in the Riverside edition, (Plate 9), in which Aaron the Moor, by virtue of his intense blackness and physical position, stands alone. Othello's blackness is not only a mark of his physical alienation but a symbol, to which every character in the play, himself included, must respond. The potential impact of his physical appearance upon audiences is suggested by Charles Lamb's frank admission that although he could find Othello admirable in the reading he was only repelled by the figure of a "*coal-black Moor*" on stage; he concluded that the play should be read, not seen. According to Margaret Webster, modern audiences were stunned more constructively by the first appearance of Paul Robeson in the role: "Here was a great man, a man of simplicity and strength; here also was a black man. We believed that he could command the armies of Venice; we knew that he would always be alien to its society."

The most dramatic reactions to Othello's blackness within the play are those of Iago and Roderigo in the opening scene. Their overt and vicious racism provides the background for Othello's first appearance. For Iago Othello is "an old black ram" (I.i.88), "the devil" (I.i.91), and a "Barbary horse" (I.i.111); the consummation of his marriage is a making of "the beast with two backs" (I.i.115–16). Roderigo, who shares Iago's disgust, speaks of Desdemona's "gross revolt" (I.i.134) and the "gross clasps of a lascivious Moor" (I.i.126). As Jones and Hunter have shown, these characters evoke, in a few choice epithets, the reigning stereotype of the African on the Elizabethan stage. Othello is black, and his blackness connotes ugliness, treachery, lust, bestiality, and the demonic. This poisonous image of the black man, as we shall see, later informs Othello's judgment of himself. Although Iago's notorious artistry is usually linked to his capacity to shape a plot, it extends as well to characterization, for the Othello he in many ways creates comes to see himself as his own stereotype.

Although he lacks Iago's sardonic wit, Brabantio shares his imagery of blackness, for his rage at Othello expresses the same racism Iago and Roderigo had incited in the streets of Venice. Brabantio has often entertained Othello and, with

Desdemona, listened to his tales. Yet the discovery that his daughter has married the Moor releases in him violent feelings of fear, hatred, and disgust. He accuses Othello of being a "foul thief," of being "damned," of arousing Desdemona's love by witchcraft (I.ii.62), of working against her by "practices of cunning hell" (I.iii.102), of being a bond-slave and pagan (I.ii.99). At the root of his amazement and outrage is physical revulsion; he cannot believe that his daughter would "run from her guardage to the sooty bosom / Of such a thing as thou—to fear, not to delight!" (I.ii.70–71). This sense of Othello as a revolting object, a "thing," recurs with tragic irony at the end of the play, when Lodovico turns away from the corpses of Othello and Desdemona on the marriage bed and orders, "The object poisons sight, / Let it be hid" (V.ii.364–65). The tragic culmination of Othello's repulsiveness is a sight that must be hidden.

Emilia is an even subtler study in latent racist feeling than Brabantio. Up to the point of the murder, she never alludes to Othello's race; nor is her relationship to him in any way remarkable. She serves her lady, commiserates with her when her marriage turns sour, defends her against Othello's attacks, and generalizes her frustration with him into cynical comments about all men. When Othello confronts her with his murder of Desdemona, however, she explodes with suppressed racial hatred:

> *Othello:* She's like a liar gone to burning hell:
> 'Twas I that killed her.
> *Emilia:* O, the more angel she,
> And you the blacker devil! (V.ii.129–31)

Even though the emotion of the moment centers upon the fact of the murder, what Emilia reveals about herself in the use of the word "blacker" is startling. Her cynical attitude towards men has apparently masked a revulsion against Othello's blackness. Having exposed his evil, Othello becomes for her a "blacker devil," the phrase revealing that in her imagination he has always been a black devil. He also becomes Desdemona's "most filthy bargain" (V.ii.157), a creature "as ignorant as dirt" (V.ii.164). As she learns more about Iago's responsibility for the crime, Emilia becomes less violent in her outrage—Othello becomes more fool than devil—but she dies with no change in these feelings of abhorrence and contempt. Her savage and reductive outburst of racist feeling at this crucial moment in the play enables audiences to vent and, ideally, to exorcise their own latent hostility, as well as their suspicions that Othello would eventually conform to type. Emilia's violent reductivism may enhance an audience's awareness, even at this point in the play, of Othello's humanity.

Desdemona loves Othello and dies defending him against the charge of her own murder. Yet she is perhaps the subtlest victim of Venetian racism. Brabantio ascribes her love to witchcraft because he cannot believe that she could otherwise overcome the horror of Othello's blackness—"and she, in spite of nature, / Of years, of country, credit, every thing, / To fall in love with what she fear'd to look on!" (I.iii.96–98). Brabantio's imputation of fear in Desdemona may be in part a projection of his own emotion, but Othello himself later confirms her reaction when he agrees with Iago's assertion that she "seem'd to shake and fear your looks" (III.iii.207). Desdemona too provides implicit confirmation when she tells the Duke "I saw Othello's visage in his mind" (I.iii.252). This implicit denial of physical attraction shows that Desdemona tries to separate Othello's essential humanity from his appearance, but it also shows that she is sensitive to and disquieted by the insinuations that there must be something unnatural in such a love. She does not say that she found Othello's blackness beautiful but that she saw his visage in his mind.

—Edward Berry, "Othello's Alienation," *Studies in English Literature 1500–1900* 30, No. 2 (Spring 1990): 318–21

✤

JULIA GENSTER ON POWER IN *OTHELLO*

[Julia Genster is a professor of English at Connecticut College. In this extract, Genster examines the degree to which military rank is an emblem of both social and sexual power in *Othello*.]

In its treatment of military offices, with their ordinal structures and their real and emblematic functions, *Othello* is consistently alive to the ways in which these offices give rise to certain orderings of perception, for the characters within the drama and for the audience without. Arrangements and rearrangements of power—political, social, sexual—are, amid what Frank Whigham has called the "surge of social mobility that occurred at the boundaries between ruling and subject classes in late sixteenth-century England," a habitual Shakespearean concern. The exact configurations of military power are not. M. R. Ridley reminds us that "Shakespeare's use of military rank is both limited and loose." And yet in *Othello* arrangements of social and sexual power are played out particularly close to the terms of office, of place. Who occupies what offices, military and sexual, how long and how well they hold them, how they gain or lose them: these questions arise so frequently in the drama that they become a kind of ideational tic—a tic which all the characters touch upon, but which Iago palpates with cunning, expert, obsessive urgency. What interests Iago, what interests Shakespeare, are the ways in which the ranks that place soldiers in legible relation to one another may be mapped on to the structures of personal identity, of social and sexual governance.

The metaphoric dovetailing of sexual and military orders is a Renaissance commonplace, as writers probe the Petrarchan vocabulary of erotic attitudes. But *Othello* suggests what we do not find suggested to the same degree elsewhere in Shakespeare's works: the ways that particular military offices with their attendant duties may be made to constitute emblematic and rhetorical places, which are then inscribed upon other structures, domestic or social. All of the play's characters are interested in the possibilities that the different networks may be brought into correspondence, but Iago is the most adept reader in and reader out of place inscriptions. Recasting the clown's riddling in Iago's terms, to tell where a person lodges in one structure is to tell where he may be belied in, dislodged from, another.

In Iago's and in the play's preoccupation with military places as loci for rhetorical invention and particularly in the office whose assignment is the most frequently interrogated—that of the lieutenancy—Shakespeare presents a figure, an image, which provides a vantage point on the play. (The word appears 26 times in *Othello,* which makes it half as frequent as "honest.") In this drama where "all relations are embedded in power and sexuality," lieutenancy, in its definition, its practice, its very etymology, extends its force over the play as a whole.

As that etymology reminds us, the lieutenant is the place holder for his commanding officer. The lieutenant is at once a sign of his commander's power and a powerful reminder of his potential absence, since the lieutenant either receives the commands of his superior officer or substitutes for him. In choosing a subordinate a captain is, in effect, choosing a second self; he is empowering someone to play him, to be him in his absence. In *Othello* the image is most ferocious when it provides the putative cuckold with the emblem of his own cuckolding: someone unauthorized is standing in for him, holding his place, doing his office. Yet the cuckold is present, imaginatively, watching as the adulterous lover displaces him. He is both present and usurped, as Iago's sharpened pun makes clear: "Would you, the supervisor, grossly gape on, / Behold her topp'd?" (3.3.401–402). In the ocular proof that Iago offers to his mind's eye, Othello is both supervisor, Cassio's commander, and yet as supervisor, overseer, doubly impotent. The cuckold's mind is haunted by the figure of his own absence from the pictures so powerfully present to his imagination.

Lieutenancy appears here at its most obvious and most corrosive, as it collapses military and domestic structures. It describes more generally, however, a suggestive angle on Iago's mind and the power that he is able to exercise over the play's other characters, and on the competition between Iago and Desdemona for Othello and for us. Lieutenancy thus thematizes that potential collapse of different structures of signification into one another; for the characters within the drama it figures both their hopes and their terrors; for the audience it patterns their engagement and their defense.

—Julia Genster, "Lieutenancy, Standing In, and *Othello,*" *ELH* 57, No. 4 (Winter 1990): 785–86

Derek Cohen on Othello's Suicide

[Derek Cohen is a professor of English at York University and the author of *Shakespearean Motives* (1988) and *Shakespeare's Culture* (1993). In this extract, Cohen analyzes the social, political, and cultural issues surrounding Othello's suicide.]

Othello's suicide engages a knotty complex of social, political and cultural issues. Far from resolving the political and cultural dilemmas of the drama, it exacerbates them and raises more questions than it answers. In that extended moment, his dagger poised to strike himself, Othello drags into the play a memory buried deep in his pre-play past that is of such brutality and hate-filled violence as to link this so-called 'restored' Othello with the crude, tortured brute who struck his wife in act IV, scene i rather than with the noble Roman he exhorts his audience to remember.

The malignant and turbanned Turk exists as a remembered victim of the Moor. The words 'smote him thus' bring Othello into a definitive identification *with* his former victim, murdered for beating a Venetian and traducing, we presume, the *Venetian* state in his (the Turk's) own city of Aleppo. Othello, the black Moor, once murdered a black Turk for 'traducing' the white Venetian state in the black city of Aleppo. (I use the racial terms black and white in their current sense, which I take to be little different from their seventeenth-century sense.) This Turk has a history; he is, in short, more than merely an enabling figure of the suicide. He possessed an identity separate and different from Othello. He was circumcised; he wore a turban; he was violent; he was stronger than the Venetian he beat and less strong than Othello; he hated the Venetian state; he was stabbed to death by Othello. As a Moor, Othello was circumcised, once wore a turban, and once, perhaps, 'traduced' the Venetian state before becoming its servant.

In Othello's suicide an intense drama of self-hatred is played out. Instead of restoring his morally and emotionally battered self, the suicide is a culmination of the assault made on him by the contending political and psychological stresses that have been brought into play. Othello and *Othello* can be seen as the complete triumph of the white world's ethos of individualism. The black man/character, separated by nature from the white hegemonic civilization, is whirled and buffeted by confusion and contradiction. He is loved and feared for his warriorship, but hated and feared for his colour.

The dichotomies suggested by the black-and-white facts and images of the play establish a dramatic world and political structure whose vocabulary tends to sustain literality and monologic interpretation. No one in the play is more susceptible to this mode of thought than Othello himself. It is and has been a means of evasion necessary for his survival as a participant in the white world who has betrayed the people he was brought up with. Othello is presented as a willing instrument of white domination and a credulous, enabling tool of white civilization. He is used by the Venetian state to sustain that domination against its black enemies. *Othello* uses Othello to support another of the pillars of white domination, that of the dangers of miscegenation.

The final and total success of white culture is contained in the single abusive phrase 'the circumcised dog,' which reaffirms a *white* construction of the remembered event. No doubt or hesitation informs Othello's recollection. On the contrary, the relish with which he recovers his own ambiguous blackness through the agency of suicide only serves to reify and intensify the colour divisions of the drama. It is no accident that Othello is referred to as 'the Moor' far more often than as Othello. For whatever the situation, Othello's colour and foreignness are the immediate means of situating him in relation to the play's other characters. He is always different. Martin Orkin, in line with a majority of critics of the play, argues that the racist sentiment in the play is confined to Iago, Roderigo, and Brabantio. This kind of analysis, however, depends entirely upon verbal construction. Simply, the racial sentiments of other characters are not tested. Polite racism, a speciality of Western industrial societies, precisely forbids the verbal expression of racist sentiment during the practice of racial discrimination. The result is an appearance of racial justice without the inconvenience to white domination that this would entail. In South Africa, to use an egregious but pertinent example, the moral justification of apartheid always hinged on the proposition that the races should be kept 'separate but equal.' Equality was desirable because fair; but separateness, on a host of religious, ethnic, political, psychological grounds, was the essence of the ideology. 'Separate but equal' was recognized by some to be a contradiction in terms, but the managers of apartheid adhered tenaciously to the slogan, creating a polity of separateness that is anything but equal. In *Othello,* it is this same notion that is teased and worried by the white Venetians in their contemplations of the black warrior. The play, as many a critic has noted, is full of the evidence and rhetoric of racial tolerance; evidence of how Othello is *accepted* by the white world. The most famous of such evidence is also the phoniest: 'I think this tale would win my daughter too.' This is lip-service of a supersubtle kind which plays into as it acknowledges the existence of a complex racial politics of dominance and submission. Shakespeare has hit upon the pivotal issue of racial relations—miscegenation. Saying, as the duke does, that one's daughter might have been seduced by the gorgeous rhetoric of a married man is no more than a declaration of admiration for his rhetoric—that is, it is perfectly safe to say it. The duke's identification with Brabantio is hollow. And yet the question of the taboo against racial mixing is given a new, sharp focus by this intervention. For the most contradictory and complex social taboo in Western societies is the taboo against interracial marriage. It is especially strong in constructions of fathers contemplating the marriages of their daughters to black men whose sexual potency is an essential part of white racial mythology. The myth is paradoxically designed to repel white women—black men are sexually insatiable and a woman who sleeps with one is feeding her baser, animal passions.

At the outset, it is clear that the state has nothing to fear from Othello while he has much to fear from it. For the demand on Othello for conformity is greater than it is for any other character; the evident penalty for non-conformity is hazard and difficulty, as his courtship of and marriage to Desdemona show. Those critical and theatrical attempts (Jonathan Miller's BBC *Othello* comes to mind) to make Othello almost white, arab rather than negro, dusky rather than brown, are themselves examples of the racism that they sometimes attempt to condemn. Racial difference is a ubiquitous problem. No character does not refer to Othello's racial difference and separateness. Such references, however apparently benign, fulfil one of the chief dogmas of white domination. They always reconstruct difference and separateness; they always put a schism between Othello and the white power structure. Thus even benignity—like the duke's—on racial matters in a situation where Othello poses no threat is automatically self-serving. While Othello conforms to state politics and state racial policy, he is allowed to be secure. While he continues, in other words, to regard the world of black, circumcised men as his enemy, he is the darling of the state. When, however, he breaches this politics, he increases his own danger in and to the Venetian state. Venice is stronger in having a black general to fight a black enemy. Just as the fact of the American military being led by a black general in, say, Grenada or Iraq, is by itself a powerful statement about the American state: it ends up sustaining the value of white power in the world while it simultaneously promotes the idea of racial equality. Othello's function is rhetorically similar.

—Derek Cohen, "Othello's Suicide," *University of Toronto Quarterly* 62, No. 3 (Spring 1993): 323–25

JAMES R. AUBREY ON MONSTER IMAGERY AND RACISM IN *OTHELLO*

[James R. Aubrey is a professor of English at the Metropolitan State College of Denver. He has written *John Fowles: A Reference Companion* (1991). In this extract, Aubrey looks at the racist conventions existing at the time Shakespeare wrote *Othello*.]

Near the end of *The Tempest,* Antonio jests that the monster Caliban "is a plain fish, and no doubt marketable." As an earlier remark in the play makes clear, however, Caliban would be valuable not only in a fishmarket but also as an exotic creature for display at court, "a present for any emperor that ever trod on neat's leather." When Shakespeare was writing *Othello,* his attraction to Cinthio's narrative about a black Moor in Venice may likewise have been a playwright's recognition that Othello's skin color would give him a "marketable," spectacular charge on the stage, as a character whose appearance marked him as Other, as having originated somewhere beyond the boundaries of the familiar. Although blacks had appeared on stage in earlier English plays, such roles were still extraordinary in 1604, when *Othello* was probably first performed. The opening scene of the play further exoticizes Othello with its references to him not by name but as "the Moor," and as an "extravagant and wheeling stranger" (1.1.58 and 1.1.37). Blacks were outsiders in a more profound sense as well, at this time, for they were associated in the popular imagination with monsters, so that the play's numerous references to monstrosity would have resonated with Othello's racial characteristics to establish his extreme difference from typical Europeans. Whether some biographical Shakespeare actually considered such ideas "marketable" is not a question I can answer, but I will show that Othello's character is constructed in a way that would have engaged such popular associations of blacks with monsters and thereby would have intensified audience responses to early performances.

From the thirteenth century, monstrous races were increasingly reported to be living in Africa rather than in Asia, as Rudolf Wittkower notes. Other critics have suggested that the English in the early 1600s still thought of blacks much as they thought of monsters, as strange creatures from outside the boundaries of the known world. Michael Neill touches the issue when he discusses linkage between blackness and moral monstrosity. Emily C. Bartels locates Othello's power as a character partly in the audience's perception of his racial difference, on the basis of which people "demonize an Other as a means of securing the self." Karen Newman asserts that there is a cultural association of blacks with monsters: by virtue of his color, "Othello is a monster in the Renaissance sense of the word." Although precise attitudes in the early seventeenth century are not recoverable, documents from that time can enable us to understand more about what constituted this "Renaissance sense" of Othello's monstrousness.

The most useful evidence is, of course, contemporaneous with *Othello*. An example is the pamphlet translated in 1605 by Edward Gresham, who summarizes the contents in an arresting title:

> *Strange fearful & true news, which happened at Carlstadt, in the kingdom of Croatia. Declaring how the sun did shine like blood nine days together, and how two armies were seen in the Air, the one encountering the other. And how also a Woman was delivered of three prodigious sons, which Prophesied many strange & fearful things, which should shortly come to pass.*

Whether or not Gresham's London bookseller believed the report to be true, he evidently believed that there was a paying readership for such "news" and sold it with a cover illustration just as sensational as the contents. The cover visually represents the battle in the air and the three "prodigious sons," described inside as follows: "The first of these Prodigious Children had four heads, which spoke and uttered strange things. The second Child was black like a Moor, and the third Child like unto Death." Depicted as fully grown and articulate, these newly-born "children" prophesy eventual defeat of the Turks and a time of dearth "both here and in other places." Devout buyers no doubt took the pamphlet seriously; others probably bought it for the kind of textual pleasures available today from supermarket tabloids. The predicted conflict in Croatia may seem ironic to historians of the late twentieth century, but of more historical interest is the cover's use of black skin as a sign of monstrosity, indeed, as the child's only monstrous characteristic.

Social anthropologists would say that this idea, that blacks and monsters are related, if not equated, on some level of the popular imagination, constituted part of early modern London's "habitus," what Pierre Bourdieu defines as "a system of lasting, transposable dispositions which, integrating past experiences, functions at every moment as a *matrix of perceptions, appreciations, and actions,*" or more simply, "a socially constituted system of cognitive and motivating structures." If there was a social disposition in 1604–5 to regard blacks and monsters as similar manifestations of the Other, as *Strange News* implies that there was, such a disposition would have affected both the generation and the reception of *Othello* at that historical moment. Indeed, as parts of the same habitus, each text simultaneously reflected and reinforced that very mental linkage. ⟨. . .⟩

It is hard to imagine that Shakespeare is not deliberately exploiting such Anglo-centrism in the way he prepares an audience for Othello's entrance. In the first scene, Iago awakens Brabantio with the cry that "an old black ram / Is tupping your white ewe" (1.1.89–90)—an image of Othello and Desdemona intended to horrify her father. Iago next represents their sexual union as "your daughter cover'd with a Barbary horse" (1.1.112). Desdemona's imagined mating with an African animal is the kind of act which Paré describes among the causes of monsters, a "copulation with beasts" that leads to "the confusion of seed of diverse kinds" (25.982). Reminding her father that Othello and Desdemona may be generating monsters, Iago further baits Brabantio, "you'll have your nephews neigh to you," then reinforces the idea with a final image of Othello and Desdemona during sexual intercourse with the conventional figure of "the beast with two backs" (1.1.112–18). The first scene of the play thus prepares an audience verbally for the entrance of some "thing" that is not-human; that this "Barbary horse" will turn out to be more human than Iago—who initially seems to be the audience's kinsman—is an irony that can prove as unsettling as Gulliver's discovery that Houyhnhnms behave like people and the creatures that look like himself behave like animals.

—James R. Aubrey, "Race and the Spectacle of the Monstrous in *Othello*," *CLIO* 22, No. 3 (1993): 221–23, 227

Books by William Shakespeare

Venus and Adonis. 1593.

The Rape of Lucrece. 1594.

Henry VI. 1594.

Titus Andronicus. 1594.

The Taming of the Shrew. 1594.

Romeo and Juliet. 1597.

Richard III. 1597.

Richard II. 1597.

Love's Labour's Lost. 1598.

Henry IV. 1598.

The Passionate Pilgrim. 1599.

A Midsummer Night's Dream. 1600.

The Merchant of Venice. 1600.

Much Ado about Nothing. 1600.

Henry V. 1600.

The Phoenix and the Turtle. 1601.

The Merry Wives of Windsor. 1602.

Hamlet. 1603.

King Lear. 1608.

Troilus and Cressida. 1609.

Sonnets. 1609.

Pericles. 1609.

Othello. 1622.

Mr. William Shakespeares Comedies, Histories & Tragedies. Ed. John Heminge and Henry Condell. 1623 (First Folio), 1632 (Second Folio), 1663 (Third Folio), 1685 (Fourth Folio).

Poems. 1640.

Works. Ed. Nicholas Rowe. 1709. 6 vols.

Works. Ed. Alexander Pope. 1723–25. 6 vols.

Works. Ed. Lewis Theobald. 1733. 7 vols.

Works. Ed. Thomas Hanmer. 1743–44. 6 vols.

Works. Ed. William Warburton. 1747. 8 vols.

Plays. Ed. Samuel Johnson. 1765. 8 vols.

Plays and Poems. Ed. Edmond Malone. 1790. 10 vols.

The Family Shakespeare. Ed. Thomas Bowdler. 1807. 4 vols.

Works. Ed. J. Payne Collier. 1842–44. 8 vols.

Works. Ed. H. N. Hudson. 1851–56. 11 vols.

Works. Ed. Alexander Dyce. 1857. 6 vols.

Works. Ed. Richard Grant White. 1857–66. 12 vols.

Works (Cambridge Edition). Ed. William George Clark, John Glover, and William Aldis Wright. 1863–66. 9 vols.

A New Variorum Edition of the Works of Shakespeare. Ed. H. H. Furness et al. 1871– .

Works. Ed. W. J. Rolfe. 1871–96. 40 vols.

The Pitt Press Shakespeare. Ed. A. W. Verity. 1890–1905. 13 vols.

The Warwick Shakespeare. 1893–1938. 13 vols.

The Temple Shakespeare. Ed. Israel Gollancz. 1894–97. 40 vols.

The Arden Shakespeare. Ed. W. J. Craig, R. H. Case et al. 1899–1924. 37 vols.

The Shakespeare Apocrypha. Ed. C. F. Tucker Brooke. 1908.

The Yale Shakespeare. Ed. Wilbur L. Cross, Tucker Brooke, and Willard Highley Durham. 1917–27. 40 vols.

The New Shakespeare (Cambridge Edition). Ed. Arthur Quiller-Couch and John Dover Wilson. 1921–62. 38 vols.

The New Temple Shakespeare. Ed. M. R. Ridley. 1934–36. 39 vols.

Works. Ed. George Lyman Kittredge. 1936.

The Penguin Shakespeare. Ed. G. B. Harrison. 1937–59. 36 vols.

The New Clarendon Shakespeare. Ed. R. E. C. Houghton. 1938– .

The Arden Shakespeare. Ed. Una Ellis-Fermor et al. 1951– .

The Complete Pelican Shakespeare. Ed. Alfred Harbage. 1969.

The Complete Signet Classic Shakespeare. Ed. Sylvan Barnet. 1972.

The Oxford Shakespeare. Ed. Stanley Wells. 1982– .

The New Cambridge Shakespeare. Ed. Philip Brockbank. 1984– .

Works about William Shakespeare and *Othello*

Adamson, Jane. *Othello as Tragedy: Some Problems of Judgment and Feeling.* Cambridge: Cambridge University Press, 1980.

Adamson, W. A. "Unpinned or Undone?: Desdemona's Critics and the Problem of Sexual Innocence." *Shakespeare Studies* 13 (1980): 169–86.

Amneus, Daniel. *The Three Othellos.* Alhambra, CA: Primrose Press, 1986.

Bartels, Emily C. "Making More of the Moor: Aaron, Othello, and Renaissance Refashionings of Race." *Shakespeare Quarterly* 41 (1990): 433–54.

Bloom, Harold, ed. *Iago.* New York: Chelsea House, 1992.

———, ed. *William Shakespeare's* Othello. New York: Chelsea House, 1987.

Bradshaw, Graham. "Obeying the Time in *Othello:* A Myth and the Mess It Made." *English Studies* 73 (1992): 211–28.

Braxton, Phyllis Natalie. "*Othello:* The Moor and the Metaphor." *South Atlantic Review* 55 (1990): 1–17.

Bulman, James C. *The Heroic Idiom of Shakespearean Tragedy.* Newark: University of Delaware Press, 1985.

Calderwood, James L. *The Properties of* Othello. Amherst: University of Massachusetts Press, 1989.

Colie, Rosalie. *Shakespeare's Living Art.* Princeton: Princeton University Press, 1974.

Cook, Ann Jennalie. "The Design of Desdemona: Doubt Raised and Resolved." *Shakespeare Studies* 13 (1980): 187–96.

Elliott, Martin. *Shakespeare's Invention of Othello.* New York: St. Martin's Press, 1988.

Everett, Barbara. *Young Hamlet: Essays on Shakespeare's Tragedies.* Oxford: Clarendon Press, 1989.

Felperin, Howard. *Shakespearean Representation.* Princeton: Princeton University Press, 1977.

Gohlke, Madelon. " 'I Wooed Thee with My Sword': Shakespeare's Tragic Paradigms." In *The Woman's Part: Feminist Criticism of Shakespeare,* ed. Carolyn Ruth Swift Lenz, Gayle Green, and Carol Thomas Neely. Urbana: University of Illinois Press, 1980.

———. " 'All That Is Spoke Is Marred': Language and Consciousness in *Othello.*" *Women's Studies* 9 (1981–82): 157–76.

Greene, Gayle. " 'This That You Call Love': Sexual and Social Tragedy in *Othello.*" *Journal of Women's Studies in Literature* 1 (1979): 16–32.

Hollindale, Peter. "Othello and Desdemona." *Critical Survey* 1 (1989): 43–52.

Kahn, Coppélia. *Man's Estate: Masculine Identity in Shakespeare.* Berkeley: University of California Press, 1981.

Kirsch, Arthur. *Shakespeare and the Experience of Love.* Cambridge: Cambridge University Press, 1981.

Little, Arthur L., Jr. " 'An Essence That's Not Seen': The Primal Scene of Racism in *Othello.*" *Shakespeare Quarterly* 44 (1993): 304–24.

McBride, Tom. "Othello's Orotund Occupation." *Texas Studies in Literature and Language* 30 (1988): 412–30.

McElroy, Bernard. "*Othello:* The Visage in His Mind." In *Shakespeare's Mature Tragedies.* Princeton: Princeton University Press, 1973, pp. 89–144.

McPherson, David C. *Shakespeare, Jonson, and the Myth of Venice.* Newark: University of Delaware Press, 1990.

Mason, H. A. *Shakespeare's Tragedies of Love.* New York: Barnes & Noble, 1970.

Mikesell, Margaret Lael, and Virginia Mason Vaughan, comp. *Othello: An Annotated Bibliography.* New York: Garland, 1990.

Miola, Robert S. "Othello Furens." *Shakespeare Quarterly* 41 (1990): 49–64.

Mooney, Michael E. *Shakespeare's Dramatic Transactions.* Durham, NC: Duke University Press, 1990.

Neill, Michael. "Unproper Beds: Race, Adultery, and the Hideous in *Othello.*" *Shakespeare Quarterly* 40 (1989): 383–412.

Parker, Patricia. "*Othello* and *Hamlet:* Dilation, Spying, and the 'Secret Place' of Woman." *Representations* 44 (Fall 1993): 60–95.

Rosenberg, Marvin. *The Masks of* Othello. Berkeley: University of California Press, 1961.

Shakespeare Survey 21 (1968). Special *Othello* issue.

Sharma, Vandana. "Shakespeare and the 'New' World: *Othello* and Cultural Readings." *Text and Representation* 11 (1991): 97–105.

Snow, Edward. "Sexual Anxiety and the Male Order of Things in *Othello.*" *English Literary Renaissance* 10 (1980): 385–411.

Stavropoulos, Janet C. "Love and Age in *Othello.*" *Shakespeare Studies* 19 (1987): 125–42.

Vaughan, Virginia Mason. Othello: *A Contextual History.* Cambridge: Cambridge University Press, 1994.

Vaughan, Virginia Mason, and Kent Cartwright, ed. Othello: *New Perspectives.* Rutherford, NJ: Fairleigh Dickinson University Press, 1991.

Index of Themes and Ideas